LATIN AMERICA

PEOPLES AND CULTURES SERIES

LATIN AMERICA

by JAMES I. CLARK

ML

McDougal, Littell & Company

Evanston, Illinois

New York   Dallas   Sacramento   Raleigh

JAMES I. CLARK, the author of the *Peoples and Cultures Series*, received his B.A. and M.A. in History and his Ph.D. in Education from the University of Wisconsin at Madison. He has taught social studies in elementary and high schools in Wyoming and Wisconsin, and has been an elementary and high school principal. He has also taught at Edgewood College, Madison, Wisconsin, and at the University of Wisconsin at Eau Claire. In addition, he has served as the director of social studies for two major publishing companies. He is author of over a dozen texts on world cultures and American history.

MIRIAM GREENBLATT, editorial and research consultant for the *Peoples and Cultures Series*, is the author of several texts on world history and world cultures.

DONALD H. LINDSTROM, Social Studies Coordinator for the West Aurora Schools, Illinois, is consultant for the *Peoples and Cultures Series*.

COVER

This church, home of the shrine of the Dark Lady of the Lake, was first built over Incan temples in 1550 but has been remodeled many times since. Its present architecture reflects both Spanish and Indian influence. The church is located in the Andean mountain town of Copacabana, Bolivia. Copacabana rests on the shores of Lake Titicaca, the highest navigable lake in the world, on the border between Bolivia and Peru. © Norman Prince.

BACK COVER

Traditional folk art represents the eight world areas in the *Peoples and Cultures Series*. Clockwise from the upper left: traditional Chinese symbol for happiness and longevity; fantastic bird motif from Latin America; royal elephant from an Indian wall hanging; Japanese crane motif; Islamic geometric design from the Middle East; Hmong pa ndau stitchery motif from Southeast Asia; decorated Ukrainian Easter egg (from *Ukrainian Easter Eggs* by A. Kmit, L. Luciow, J. Luciow, and L. Perchyshyn) from the Soviet Union; carved wood panel from Africa. The world map in the center, courtesy of Maryland CartoGraphics, symbolizes *Learning About Peoples and Cultures*.

Traditional folk art represents the eight world areas in the *Peoples and Cultures Series*. Clockwise from the upper left: traditional Chinese symbol for happiness and longevity; fantastic bird motif from Latin America; royal elephant from an Indian wall hanging; Japanese crane motif; Islamic geometric design from the Middle East; Hmong pa ndau stitchery motif from Southeast Asia; decorated Ukrainian Easter egg (from *Ukrainian Easter Eggs* by A. Kmit, L. Luciow, J. Luciow, and L. Perchyshyn) from the Soviet Union; carved wood panel from Africa. The world map in the center, courtesy of Maryland CartoGraphics, Inc., symbolizes *Learning About Peoples and Cultures*.

Acknowledgments: See page 167

ISBN 0-8123-5783-3

89 90 91 92 93 / 15 14 13 12 11 10 9 8 7 6 5 4 3 2 1

CONTENTS

PRONUNCIATION OF LATIN AMERICAN WORDS

Most of the foreign words used in this book are Spanish. For those unfamiliar with Spanish, the basic vowel sounds are usually long:

a as in *father*   **o** as in *note*

e like the **a** in *gate*   **u** as in *rule*

i like the first **e** in *eve*

Consonants are pronounced as they are in English, except:

b and **v** represent the same sound, which is like **b** in *bone,* at the beginning of a word or following **m** or **n**; otherwise like the **v** in *ever*

ch is like the **ch** in *church*

ge, gi, and **j** sound like the **h** in *hat,* except very strong and rasping

h is always silent, except after **c**

ll is like the **y** in *yes*

ñ is like the **ny** in *canyon*

qu followed by **e** or **i** sounds like **k**; the **u** is silent

r is trilled; **rr** is trilled with three to four vibrations

x in *México* and *mexicano* is pronounced like the **h** in *hat,* except stronger; in names of Indian origin, like an **s** or **sh**

z is like the **s** in *see*

Mayan head from Copán, Honduras.

Words that end with a vowel, or with **n** or **s**, stress the next last syllable. For example: *peso* ('pay-so), *peninsulares* (pay-neen-soo-'lah-race). Words that end with any consonant other than **n** or **s** stress the last syllable. For example: *señor* (say-'nyor). Words that are exceptions to these rules bear a written accent (') over the stressed vowel. For example, *cantón* (kan-'tōn), *político* (po-'lee-tee-ko).

Portuguese is the official language of Brazil, which holds almost one-third of the total population of Latin America. French is spoken in Haiti. In addition, millions of Latin Americans speak Indian dialects, such as Quechua and Aymará. Where possible, pronunciations for foreign words will be given in the Student's Guide.

Foreign words and phrases used in this book are italicized when first used, but not thereafter. Most of these terms are defined in the Index and Glossary.

LATIN AMERICA

UNITED STATES

Washington, D.C. ★

NORTH AMERICA

Rio Grande

San Antonio

Mississippi R.

New Orleans

GULF OF MEXICO

BAJA CALIFORNIA

MEXICO

Monterrey

Nueces R.

Guadalajara

Guanajuato

Mexico City ★   Veracruz

OAXACA   San Cristóbal   YUCATÁN

Zinacantán

GUATEMALA   HONDURAS

Guatemala City

San Salvador   EL SALVADOR

Tegucigalpa

Managua

San José   Panama City

COSTA RICA

PANAMA   CANAL ZONE (U.S.A.)

Buenaventura

Havana

CUBA

Guantánamo Bay

Port au Prince

Santiago de Cuba   San Juan   PUERTO RICO

Kingston   HAITI   Santo Domingo

JAMAICA   DOMINICAN REPUBLIC

CARIBBEAN SEA

BAHAMA IS.

ATLANTIC OCEAN

BARBADOS IS.

GRENADA IS.

TOBAGO   TRINIDAD

VENEZUELA

Caracas

Carabobo   Georgetown   GUYANA

L. de Maracaibo   Guayana   Paramaribo   SURINAM

Mt. Roraima   Cayenne   FRENCH GUIANA

Bogotá   Bôa Vista

COLOMBIA   RORAIMA

Tuluá   San Pedro   Buga

Cali

ARCH. DE COLÓN (GALÁPAGOS IS.)

Equator   Equator

ECUADOR   Quito

Negro R.   Amazon R.   Belém

Manaus

Amazon R.

Marañón R.

Recife

PERU   BRAZIL

Machu Picchu

Lima   Madeira R.   Salvador da Bahia

Cuzco   Titicaca   Brasília

BOLIVIA   São Francisco R.

La Paz   Belo Horizonte

Sucre   MINAS GERAIS

Potosí   Volta Redonda

PARAGUAY   Rio de Janeiro

São Paulo

Paraguay R.

PACIFIC OCEAN

Asunción

Paraná R.

CHILE   RIO GRANDE DO SUL

Córdoba   SOUTH AMERICA

Valparaíso   Rosario

Santiago   Uruguay R.

El Teniente   Buenos Aires   Punta del Este

Montevideo   URUGUAY

ARGENTINA   Rio de la Plata

Latin America

1000 miles   500   0

1500   1000   500   0   kilometers

FALKLAND IS. (IS. MALVINAS)

Strait of Magellan

TIERRA DEL FUEGO

Cape Horn

ANDES MOUNTAINS

CONQUEST AND RULE

About 25,000 years ago, groups of people began to move from Siberia into the Americas. What prompted their migration no one knows. Perhaps climatic change. Perhaps a shortage of game. Perhaps pressure from stronger, more aggressive peoples. In any case, they crossed the Bering Strait, which may have been land at the time or perhaps frozen over, into what is now Alaska. From there, as centuries passed, they fanned out over two continents, as far south as present-day Chile. White men who found these peoples in the Americas in the fifteenth century called them Indians.

Some Indian tribes remained nomadic, periodically moving from place to place to locate food. Others became sedentary, settling in villages and existing mostly by farming. Maize, or corn, became their main crop, and it figured in numerous ceremonies and legends. Said the Maya, a people of Central America:

> After that [the gods] began to talk about the creation and the making of our first mother and father; of yellow corn and of white corn they made their flesh; of cornmeal dough they made the arms and legs of man.

Numerous tribes filtered into Central America, where village life began between 3500 and 3000 B.C. The Olmecs developed a culture along the east coast of Mexico that flourished between 1200 and 100 B.C. Mayan culture, which flowered between the fourth and tenth centuries A.D., centered mainly on the Yucatán Peninsula. The Maya developed a hieroglyphic writing system as well as an advanced system of mathematics which, along with astronomical observations, enabled them to calculate the length of the year at 365.2420 days. More recent measurements with precision instruments place it at 365.2422 days. The Maya also built ceremonial cities, placing in their centers huge flat-topped stone pyramids on which they erected temples. Mayan culture went into decline about 800, and within a century it had disappeared.

Opposite: A bearded Mayan ruler stares down from this stone stela carved in the eighth century.

West of the Yucatán Peninsula, in the high central valley of Mexico, a people known as Aztecs gradually assumed control over several Indian tribes. The Aztecs seem to have entered the central valley from the northwest in the twelfth or thirteenth century, eventually settling on a rocky island in a lake named Texcoco. Beginning as a cluster of rude mud huts, the settlement called Tenochtitlán developed into a city of stone buildings and temples, probably the most splendid and impressive Indian city of the Western Hemisphere. Connected to the mainland by broad causeways, Tenochtitlán held 300,000 people by the early 1500s. A Spaniard who viewed it at that time wrote:

> The great city of Tenochtitlán has and had many wide and handsome streets. Of these, two or three are the principal streets, and all the others are formed half of hard earth like a brick pavement, and the other half of water, so that the people can go out along the land or by water in the boats and canoes which are made of hollowed wood, and some are large enough to hold five persons. The inhabitants go abroad some by water in these boats and others by land, and they can talk to one another as they go. There are other principal streets in addition, entirely of water, which can only be traversed by boats and canoes, as is their wont, as I have already said, for without these boats they could neither go in nor out of their houses.

The Aztec empire began small but expanded under Montezuma I, who reigned from 1440 to 1469. The Aztecs won control over peoples to the southwest and peoples in the humid lowland areas along the east coast. Eventually their empire stretched from coast to coast and from the desert regions in the north almost to Guatemala in the south. The Aztecs forced conquered peoples to accept their gods and to pay tribute. This frequently took the form of maize and other foods and cotton cloth.

Although fierce warriors, physically the Aztecs were unimpressive. Few men topped five feet six inches in height. Women averaged about four feet eight. The hair of both sexes was coarse, straight, and black. "They are swarthy as leopards, of good manners and gestures, for the greater part very skillful, robust, and tireless, and at the same time the most moderate men known," wrote a Spaniard who observed them. Basic everyday Aztec dress for both men and women was a loincloth, tied so that the ends hung down in front and back. Ceremonial clothing was

Opposite: The swaying figure of a dancer bearing a baton and a fan. Peruvian Indians of a pre-Inca culture used these embroidered cloths to wrap their dead.

much more elaborate, and so was that of nobles and the ruling family.

PYRAMID OF AZTEC POWER

At the peak of the Aztec social and political pyramid stood the ruler, usually spoken of as king or chief of men. He was an exclusive sort, seldom appearing before his subjects. When he traveled, he rested on a litter carried by noblemen. Noblemen chose rulers by election. After the founding of Tenochtitlán, they were all selected from a single family.

The Aztec king held absolute power. Montezuma II, who reigned in the early 1500s, possessed a personal guard of two hundred chieftains. Only a few of them were permitted to speak to the king. None was allowed to look him directly in the face, nor were any but a select few persons admitted to an audience with him. He dined grandly from gold plates and cups, served always by two handsome women. Montezuma II was described in 1520 as

about forty years old, well-proportioned, spare and slight, and not very dark, though of the usual Indian complexion. He did not wear his hair long, but just over his ears, and he had a short black beard, well-shaped and thin. His face was rather long and cheerful, he had fine eyes, and in his appearance and manner could express geniality or, when necessary, a serious composure.

The king was neat and clean, said the observer, bathing every afternoon.

Below the ruler was an Aztec nobility. It

consisted of senior generals, heads of such civil service branches as the tribute collecting agency, judges, rulers of conquered peoples, and governors of various districts. Next came free commoners, organized in groups or clans called *calpulli*. They included craftsmen, tradesmen, and peasants. Slaves occupied the bottom rung of the ladder; they were used as household servants, laborers, and porters.

Most slaves were captives taken in war. Some were part of a subject people's tribute to the Aztecs. Some persons became slaves for failing to pay their debts. Others were enslaved upon conviction for such crimes as theft. Slavery was governed by law. An enslaved person's status was not hereditary. His children went free. No well-behaved slave could be sold without his consent. One who was dishonest, who did not perform tasks diligently, or who was consistently disobedient, however, had no say as to how his master might dispose of him.

Peasants labored without draft animals—such as horses or oxen—and without plows. To plant crops, they used a digging stick to prepare a hole into which they dropped seeds. In the humid tropical areas along the east coast, peasants followed what is known as slash-and-burn agriculture. They felled trees and cleared brush, then burned the debris to clear land for planting. Once the soil was exhausted—and maize in particular drained nutrients from the soil quickly—peasants moved to hack out a new village site and new farmland from the forest. Where the climate was favorable for it, peasants grew cotton along with food.

Peoples of the Aztec culture knew the principle of the wheel. Wheeled toys uncovered from Aztec ruins demonstrate this. But they did not adapt the wheel to transportation purposes. No American Indian group did, al-

Far left: An Aztec sculpture of a young warrior deity.

Left: An Inca goblet of painted wood in the form of a jaguar's head.

Right: Drinking vessels of painted pottery used by Mochica Indians, a pre-Inca group from northern Peru.

though some, like the Aztecs, built roads. The lack of draft animals was probably one reason for the absence of wheeled vehicles.

Ranking above the peasantry, a host of craftsmen served town and city populations. Stonemasons were in demand to shape materials for temples and public buildings. Weavers and tailors produced cloth and clothing, particularly for ceremonial occasions. Featherworkers were a special craft group. They made costumes and elaborate headdresses for members of the Aztec court. Coppersmiths turned out chisels and axes, fishhooks and drill bits. Other smiths worked with gold and silver, found in abundance in the land of the Aztecs, to produce ornaments and jewelry as well as cups, plates, and vases. Gold and silver held no other value for the Aztecs. They did not use those metals as a medium of exchange, that is, as money.

NOURISHING THE GODS

Sacred celebrations were of particular importance to the Aztecs. Much of their culture revolved around religion. Wrote one observer:

There was not a single act of public or private life which was not colored by religious sentiment. Religion was the [most important] factor, and . . . cause in those activities which to us seem most alien to religious feeling, such as sports, games and war. It controlled commerce, politics, conquest. It [entered] in every act of the individual, from birth until the moment when the priests cremated his corpse and interred [buried] the ashes.

The Aztecs worshipped numerous gods. Their ceremonies consisted mainly of asking the gods to influence the weather and other natural forces so as to favor all the people. The Aztecs wished particularly to ward off evil or disastrous events. Their most important god was Huitzilopochtli, a warrior deity and son of the Earth Goddess. According to Aztec legend, Huitzilopochtli had thrown himself into the fire at "the place where the gods were made" and was transformed into the sun. Other gods followed Huitzilopochtli, changing into the moon and stars. The Aztecs believed themselves to be Huitzilopochtli's chosen people. Quetzalcoatl—the patron of corn, art, and learning—was another prominent god.

Gods, the Aztecs believed, must remain strong and vigorous—especially the Sun God in his daily journey across the sky. Like humans, they needed nourishment. What greater gift could humans provide than life itself, particularly the human heart? Consequently, the Aztecs practiced human sacrifice, offering not just an occasional victim but, during certain ceremonies, thousands.

Most sacrificial victims were war captives, and the Aztecs waged frequent wars to gather victims for their gods. Slaves or children purchased for the purpose were also sacrificed. At the climax of certain religious ceremonies, priests seized and spread-eagled victims one by one across a low stone block. Four priests held the victim's arms and legs. A fifth then plunged a knife made of obsidian—a hard volcanic stone—into the victim's chest, cutting quickly across breastbone and ribs. The priest then wrenched out the still-palpitating heart, held it aloft for a moment, and finally placed it in an "eagle dish." Frequently the victim's blood was smeared on an image of the god to whom he had been sacrificed. The Aztecs believed that the souls of victims proceeded straight to the Paradise of the Sun.

The Aztecs were not the only American Indians to practice human sacrifice. The Aztecs, however, followed the practice more extensively and with greater diligence than any other group.

A warlike, rather bloody people, the Aztecs nonetheless developed a culture rich in temple building, crafts, and medical knowledge. Their government appears to have been well administered by a ruling class of nobles with bureaucratic underlings. The Aztec culture depended on tribute from conquered peoples. And this fact, after about a hundred years of high Aztec achievement, would contribute to their downfall. The Incas, Aztec counterparts in South America, enjoyed a similarly brief span of rule.

INCAS, PEOPLE OF THE SUN

According to legend, the Incas lived originally on the shores of clear and icy Lake Titicaca, astride the border of what are now Bolivia and Peru. Archaeologists have confirmed this as fact. Sometime around A.D. 1200 the Incas migrated north and west, settling finally in a ten-thousand-foot-high valley in the Andes Mountains. Here they built the city of Cuzco. Legend says that the Sun God, the chief Inca deity, commanded that the people move and that the son of the Sun, Manco Capac, lead the march.

Like the Aztecs, the Incas were short of stature. Life in high mountain regions, where air lacks the oxygen content it possesses at lower altitudes, caused them to develop unusual lung capacity. Drawings of Incas show them as barrel-chested people.

For years the Incas were simply one of numerous Indian groups occupying valleys in the Andes. Then in the early 1400s, almost suddenly, the Incas began to conquer and expand. Within a short time they ruled all of present-day Peru along with portions of Ecuador and Chile. Eventually the Inca empire held about 12 million people, around 25,000 residing in the city of Cuzco alone. People subject to the Incas formed the majority of the empire's population.

The word Inca held a double meaning. On the one hand it referred to a group which, like the Aztecs, made themselves a ruling elite over other Indian tribes. On the other hand, Inca meant the ruler himself, the Sapa Inca, or Only Inca.

RULE OF THE SAPA INCA

The Incas believed that the Sapa Inca was the son of the Sun God. Each Sapa Inca was a direct descendant of Manco Capac.

Although a Sapa Inca could take many wives, his principal spouse was a sister by whom he was to produce a male heir to the throne. Brother-sister marriages kept the ruling line pure.

As chief lawgiver and priest, the Inca held absolute power. His person, furthermore, was as sacred as his office. Before approaching him, a person had to remove his sandals and bow low. Never might he look the Inca directly in the face.

On his feet the Inca wore white wooden sandals. He dressed in fine clothing made of soft wool taken from the vicuña, an animal somewhat like a llama, both of which Indians of the Andes Mountains had domesticated. The Inca never wore the same clothing twice. Nor did he ever use a set of gold and silver tableware for more than one meal.

Around his head the Inca wore a band of colored cloth from which dangled a small tassel. This was to the Inca what a crown is to a king, a symbol of power and highest rank.

When holding audiences, the Inca sat on a solid gold throne resting on a platform also made of gold. The Inca also traveled on his throne, carried on a litter constructed of wood and copper and covered with thin sheets of gold and silver, transported by a dozen men.

His people believed that when the Sapa Inca died, he was "called back to the house of his father, the Sun." They held great religious ceremonies in honor of the Sun God. The Inca's body was preserved as a mummy and lodged in the Temple of the Sun in Cuzco. Then the son he had chosen to succeed him became the next Sapa Inca.

The Sapa Inca was a religious leader as well as a secular ruler. He himself conducted numerous ceremonies on behalf of the people. At planting time, for example, the Sapa Inca went out to break the ground with a digging stick. This signaled all peasants to dig up their land and plant seeds. At harvest time, led by the Inca, priests laid sacrifices of corn, animals, and flowers before the Sun God in his temple in Cuzco. The ceremonies continued for several days.

KNITTING TOGETHER AN EMPIRE

The Incas were great builders. Laying out the city of Cuzco in squares, they erected palaces, government buildings, and temples of stone. Using bronze chisels and scrapers, stonemasons shaped their materials so well that the building stones fitted snugly and securely together without mortar.

There were numerous Inca cities besides Cuzco, Quito to the north and Tumbes on the coast, for example. To connect all cities with Cuzco, the Incas constructed roads, in most places about twenty feet wide. At unusually steep locations, the roads became steps chiseled out of the rock. To continue the roads across deep gorges, the Incas built remarkable bridges made mainly of rope, secured by thick rope cables.

No wheeled vehicles moved along Inca roads. The Incas, like the Aztecs and other American Indians, did not use the wheel for transportation. Their only beast of burden was the llama, whose carrying capacity is limited to about a hundred pounds. Consequently human back and leg power moved such heavy burdens as corn, which following

the harvest was brought to storehouses for safekeeping against a possible famine.

The road system provided the ruling Incas with an excellent communication system. Working in relays, runners sped messages from city to city. A team could carry a message six hundred miles in five days. Since the Incas possessed no writing system, runners memorized their messages. The road network also served the Inca army, making it possible to move men quickly to repel invasion or put down rebellion among subject people.

In time of war the Inca army numbered as many as two hundred thousand men. Each soldier wore a wooden helmet padded with cotton and a breastplate made of quilted cotton cloth. Inca armament included slings, bows and arrows, spears, clubs, and axes.

OTHER PEOPLE OF THE EMPIRE

Most of the people subject to the Incas were peasants living in villages of huts made of mud bricks with roofs thatched with straw. Maize was the main crop in the lowlands along the Pacific Ocean and in the lower highlands. Potatoes and beans were the principal crops in the high mountain valleys. Some peasants grew cotton and most kept herds of llamas for their wool. Game from the forests and flocks of ducks provided meat.

Under Inca rule peasants had two main duties. They were to turn over a portion of their maize and other crops to the government for storage in Cuzco and other cities. In addition, peasants were to serve in the army and work in gold and silver mines and on such public projects as road and bridge building whenever ordered to.

The Inca empire was well administered. And for about a hundred years it remained secure. Early in the sixteenth century, however, the empire fell on evil days. Sapa Inca Huayna Capac sired two sons, Atahualpa and Huáscar. Contrary to custom, before he died Huayna Capac did not grant absolute power to one son only. He named Huáscar to succeed him. But he also gave Atahualpa power to rule the city of Quito and the area around it. The presence of two power bases proved disastrous for the empire.

Huáscar ordered Atahualpa to serve and obey him. Atahualpa refused. With that the War of the Brothers, a terrible civil war, began. During a year of savage fighting, thousands of men were killed. Atahualpa finally captured Huáscar, ending the war and giving the empire a new ruler.

Hardly had the wounds of Inca civil war healed when the empire was threatened by invasion. The invaders, however, were not Indians. They were Spaniards, strangers to the land, who had begun to explore the Americas some years before. They were fellow countrymen of invaders who had already conquered the Aztecs to the north.

Machu Picchu, ancient city of the Incas. Deserted and unknown for nearly four centuries, these precisely fitted granite structures were discovered in 1911 by a North American archaeologist.

THE SEARCH FOR EL DORADO

Chapter 2

Hope of gaining gold, silver, and other riches lured Spaniards across the Atlantic Ocean. They formed a vanguard of Europeans who would, during the course of the sixteenth and seventeenth centuries, explore much and claim all of the Americas for themselves.

Spanish interest in the Americas began with the voyages of Christopher Columbus. He made his first voyage in 1492. On his second voyage in 1493, he took fifteen hundred settlers with him. More colonists followed, spreading out from Santo Domingo, the first Spanish colony, to settle other islands in the Caribbean Sea. Spanish authorities granted colonists the right to hold Indians in *encomienda*. Indians granted in encomienda belonged to a settler's estate and had to work for him. In return, the settler was to feed, clothe, and shelter the Indians and see that they had an opportunity to become Christians and practice that faith. Legally Indians were not enslaved. Still, they could not leave estates. And although it was not strictly legal to do so, fathers passed on encomiendas to their sons.

Sugarcane and tobacco became important crops in the Spanish islands, which were known as the West Indies. But many settlers there had little interest in farming. They wanted more immediate riches.

Among the many words Columbus wrote about the Americas, these in particular stood out: "I tried to find out if there was gold. By signs [from Indians] I was able to make out that to the south there was a king who had great cups full." And many Spaniards who followed Columbus sought the land of El Dorado, a golden land.

Juan Ponce de León explored parts of Florida. He found no gold. He discovered only land filled with flowers, new Indian tribes, and a pleasant climate. One of his officers, Álvar Núñez Cabeza de Vaca, later traveled across Texas to the west coast of Mexico. Indians told Cabeza de Vaca about riches in cities to the north. These tales inspired Francisco Coronado to search through what are now New Mexico, Texas, Oklahoma, and Kansas. He sought Quivira, the city of gold. Coronado did not find it. Hernando de Soto explored much of what is now the southern part of the United States. He discovered the Mississippi River, but no gold. None of these explorers reaped riches. But all established claims to vast territories for Spain.

The quest for El Dorado persisted. And Hernán Cortés found a golden land in a high valley deep in Mexico.

Born in Spain, Cortés entered the University of Salamanca at age fourteen. Some accounts

Opposite: Cortés on the march to Tenochtitlán, from a Mexican codex, a manuscript book of ancient annals.

say he spent only two years there, probably studying law.

Adventure, not law, appealed to Cortés. And chances for adventure and perhaps riches lay across the sea. In 1504 Cortés joined a fleet of merchant ships bound for Santo Domingo. There he received a grant of Indians and land in encomienda. Bernal Díaz del Castillo, a soldier who later fought with Cortés, described him as "of good height and body and well proportioned and of strong limbs. Had his face been longer he would have been handsomer and his eyes had a somewhat loving glance yet grave withal."

PREPARATION FOR CONQUEST

In 1511 Cortés participated in the Spanish conquest of Cuba. Afterward he settled on that island. Although he was now fairly well off from landholding and trade, a quiet sedentary life did not please the young man. He itched for more exciting activity, for an opportunity to seek real wealth in the New World. And in 1518 he got his chance. Diego Velázquez, the governor of Cuba, named Cortés commander of a fleet to explore the Central American coast, an area Spaniards previously had visited briefly.

Cortés' expedition setting sail from Cuba to explore the coast of Yucatán. An engraving from the first publication in 1523 of Cortés' letters to Charles V reporting the conquest of the Aztecs.

Cortés himself footed most of the bill for the expedition, raising a portion of the money by mortgaging his encomienda. Then, when Velázquez decided to remove him from command, he sailed secretly from Cuba.

The expedition of eleven ships, about five hundred soldiers, and sixteen horses left Havana in February 1519. Catholic priests who wished to convert Indians to Christianity accompanied the explorers.

Touching first on the Yucatán Peninsula, where the Spaniards fought skirmishes with unfriendly Indians, Cortés proceeded north to present-day Veracruz. There he began a settlement.

By now Cortés had learned about the Aztecs of central Mexico and their king, Montezuma II. He had also gained information about the Aztec capital city of Tenochtitlán on Lake Texcoco. Cortés had gotten an inkling of the vast treasures of gold and silver the Aztecs possessed, and this sharpened his determination to move inland. He had also learned that Indian tribes along the coast, recently conquered by the Aztecs and forced to pay tribute to them, had little love for their overlords. These, as well as inland tribes, later became allies of the Spaniards.

A BEARDED GOD RETURNS

After several weeks' preparation on the coast at Veracruz, Cortés was ready to proceed inland. In August 1519 the march began, with the Spaniards accompanied by several hundred Indians.

Two weeks later, Cortés and his army entered the territory of Tlaxcala, and there they were forced to fight. The Tlaxcalans, despite several brave stands, proved no match for Spanish horses, steel swords, and especially muskets and cannon. Once defeated, the Tlaxcalans joined the Spanish and other Indian forces.

Montezuma had been kept informed of Spanish activity from the moment the Spaniards touched land on the Yucatán Peninsula. The king, however, apparently could not decide just how to meet what obviously was a grave danger to his kingdom and his power. Montezuma's representatives tried to persuade Indian tribes from siding with the Spaniards. These attempts enjoyed little success. Montezuma had an ambush prepared for the Spaniards. The invaders discovered and avoided it. An Aztec legend said that the god Quetzalcoatl, represented as white and bearded, would appear at about the time the Spaniards arrived. Montezuma thought that the white and bearded Cortés might be that god. More than anything else, the Spaniards' skill at arms and the victories they had won against great odds impressed the Aztec ruler. On more than one occasion, Montezuma's representatives insisted that the Spaniards were not to enter the immediate Aztec domain. Cortés stated, however, that he came in peace, although he demanded gold. He ignored Montezuma's demands that he halt. Montezuma finally decided to admit Cortés and his forces to Tenochtitlán. Even so, Cortés remained wary of a possible trap.

Cortés and his men—more than five thousand strong—reached Tenochititlán on November 8, 1519. They moved cautiously along a long causeway on which eight horsemen could march abreast. As they crossed a bridge, they were met by Montezuma, who welcomed Cortés as though he were a god.

Montezuma may have actually believed that Cortés was a god, or at least a representative of one. On the other hand, he may simply have tried to save face before his people, since he had been unable to stop the Spaniards' advance. No human, after all, could withstand the power of a deity. "You will be provided here with everything necessary for you and your people," Montezuma assured Cortés, "and you shall suffer no annoyance, for you are in your own house and country." Despite this welcome, Cortés remained on his guard.

REAPING A HARVEST

Montezuma now was in fact Cortés' prisoner. Upon demand Montezuma ordered gold turned over to the Spaniards. He may have hoped to buy them off. Spaniards melted down hundreds of trinkets, vases, necklaces, tumblers, and other objects and cooled them into gold bars. There was, however, no buying them off. And Spaniards had come seeking not only wealth but also religious converts.

Among Spanish leaders in the New World, the religious motive for subduing Indians equaled their lust for gold. Spaniards believed in Christianity as the only true religion. They were determined to convert those they considered heathens. Quickly realizing the central role religion played in Aztec life, Cortés saw Christianity as a useful weapon with which to subdue those Indians. He reasoned that if he could replace the gods the Aztecs worshipped with the Christian God, the task of conquest would be easier. In addition, while the Spaniards—like all soldiers of the time— were tough, rough-hewn men accustomed to cruelty and bloodshed, the Aztec practice of human sacrifice appalled them. They wished to stamp it out.

Cortés and his priests were not successful in turning the Aztecs to Christianity. The Spaniards erected a cross and a statue of the Virgin Mary before which they prayed. Priests celebrated mass. But Christianity with its idea of a single god did not appeal to the Aztecs.

Otherwise, Cortés thus far had been highly successful. Montezuma remained under control. Gold objects continued to flow in.

Diego Velázquez in faraway Cuba, however, posed a problem for Cortés. The conqueror had gone far beyond his orders. And this got him into trouble.

Cortés' instructions had been only to explore and trade. But he had founded a settlement at Veracruz where his men had elected him governor-general. Cortés had, in effect, set up his own government. Further, without consulting Velázquez, Cortés had begun the conquest of Mexico. Worse yet, he had gone over the governor's head to communicate directly with the king of Spain, Charles V. All this threatened Velázquez's authority. He sent a fleet bearing soldiers to Veracruz to bring Cortés in.

Upon hearing of the fleet's arrival, Cortés split his force. With 250 men he marched on the coastal settlement. He easily defeated Velázquez's men and many of them, hearing of Aztec riches, went over to Cortés' side.

NIGHT OF SORROWS

During Cortés' absence, the Aztecs staged a harvest dance. This was not harmful, but it alarmed Pedro de Alvarado, whom Cortés had left in command in Tenochtitlán. Alvarado interpreted the dance as a preparation for an uprising against the Spaniards. He struck without warning, his men slaughtering hundreds of Indians.

As a consequence, Cortés was not welcomed back to Tenochtitlán. And shortly thereafter, Aztec war chiefs overthrew Montezuma and chose his brother Cuitláhuac as emperor in his stead.

Led by Cuitláhuac, Aztec forces attacked the Spaniards. Cortés appealed to Montezuma for help. Although the former king agreed to speak to his people, he was now utterly without power or influence. Standing on a rooftop, Montezuma began to address crowds of Aztec warriors. They responded with a hail of stones and arrows, wounding Montezuma. Carried to shelter, but refusing to have his wounds tended or to eat, he died three days later.

Now the Spaniards attempted to escape the

city under cover of darkness on the night of June 30, 1520. The Aztecs discovered the attempted retreat and turned the darkness into *la Noche Triste,* the night of sorrows. About two-thirds of the Spaniards met death that night, many of them drowned in Lake Texcoco, dragged under by the weight of the gold bars they had insisted on taking with them.

After constant fighting, Cortés and his remaining men finally reached the mainland. There they regrouped and continued the retreat out of Aztec territory.

Ships carrying more men and additional firearms arrived at Veracruz from Spain. Welcoming the reinforcements, Cortés had his men construct thirteen small demountable ships. Then he marched back to Lake Texcoco. About 100,000 Indian enemies of the Aztecs joined him along the way. Cortés had the sections of the ships put together and, in April 1521, he launched the fleet against Tenochtitlán.

The Aztecs defended their city fiercely and with great skill and courage, battling literally to the death. One engagement cost twelve thousand Aztec dead, another cost forty thousand killed or captured. Still they fought on, desperately struggling against what they realized would be extinction if the Spaniards won. Cortés' men took Tenochtitlán street by street, canal by canal, destroying the city in the process. The end came, after ninety-three days of constant fighting, on August 13, 1521. Wrote old soldier Bernal Díaz after the last section of the city had been won:

We found the houses full of corpses, and some poor Mexicans still in them who could not move away. Their excretions were the sort of filth that thin swine pass which have been fed on nothing but grass. The city looked as if it had been plowed up. The roots of any edible greenery had been dug out, boiled, and eaten, and they

had even cooked the bark of some of the trees. There had been no live birth for a long time, because they had suffered so much from hunger and continual fighting.

Few epics in the annals of warfare compare with the Spanish conquest of Mexico or with the Aztec defense of their great city.

The Spaniards never found the gold they had lost on la Noche Triste. But there was plenty more where the first had come from. Mines were opened or extended, and gold and silver began to flow to Spain in abundance. Under Cortés' direction, Tenochtitlán, which became Mexico City, was rebuilt and fortified. Christian churches replaced Aztec centers of worship. The Aztecs now accepted Christianity, just as peoples they had conquered had accepted Aztec gods. Cortés granted Indians and land in encomienda to his soldiers. Breeding stock of cows, sheep, and pigs arrived from Spain. Within eighteen months following the conquest, Mexico was a secure and prosperous Spanish colony. Much of this resulted from Cortés' ability to govern.

The conquest of Mexico made Hernán Cortés rich and famous. But he did not enjoy unlimited power indefinitely. Fearing the conqueror's ability and popularity, the Spanish government gradually clipped his wings. By 1534 he had been replaced by a viceroy, a direct representative of the king. Cortés died in Spain on December 2, 1547, at age sixty-two, an embittered old man, broken in health.

Centuries later, Mexicans themselves enjoyed revenge of a sort on their conqueror. Statues of Cortés were broken up, the names of streets commemorating him were changed, and his palaces at Coyoacán and Cuernavaca were filled with paintings showing the Mexican version of the conquest.

Hernán Cortés had been the first to find a golden land. His reputed cousin, Francisco Pizarro, became the second.

PIZARRO GAINS AN EMPIRE

Chapter 3

Before Cortés' conquest of Mexico, Vasco Núñez de Balboa discovered a new sea. In 1513, with a few men, Balboa beat his way through jungles to the top of a mountain in Panama. From there he could see the Pacific Ocean. He claimed all the land the ocean touched for Spain.

On the eastern side of Panama, Balboa had heard about a fabulous land far to the south. Pointing to a small golden ornament, an Indian chief said to him: "If this is what you want so badly, I can tell you of a land where men eat and drink from golden vessels and where gold is as cheap as iron is with you." The chief did not say just where this great country lay. He simply told Balboa that he had to cross the mountain to the other ocean. From there, the land of gold lay many days' journey to the south.

Balboa would never see that golden land. But Francisco Pizarro, one of his soldiers, would.

No one knows much about Pizarro's early life. He was born in Spain, probably in 1471. His parents were poor and ignorant, and Pizarro never learned to read or write. As a young man he became a soldier. About 1510, when he was forty years old, Pizarro sailed to the Americas, hoping to make his fortune.

For several years Pizarro fought bravely against Indians and helped add more land to the Spanish empire. But great fortune eluded him. He had not become rich and famous like his relative Cortés. His efforts had gained him little more than scars from battle wounds. Pizarro still hoped to strike it rich. But time was running out. He was growing old.

As a member of Balboa's force, Pizarro had heard about the golden land south of Panama. He determined to find it.

This proved an immensely difficult task. Pizarro led two expeditions south from Panama, only to meet great hardship and utter failure. He finally succeeded on his third try, in 1530.

Landing north of Tumbes, Pizarro moved southward with about two hundred men and twenty-seven horses. Their objective was the Inca city of Cajamarca, high in the mountains. There Sapa Inca Atahualpa and his army lay encamped.

Reaching Cajamarca, Pizarro sent envoys to Atahualpa, who agreed to come to the city the next day to visit Pizarro. Then the Spaniards prepared an ambush. As Pizarro and Atahualpa talked, Pizarro suddenly gave a signal and his men attacked. The Spaniards killed two thousand unarmed Incas and captured Atahualpa.

The Inca army would not try to rescue the Sapa Inca unless he ordered an attack. He did

Opposite: Manco Capac (left), legendary founder of the Inca dynasty, and Mama Ocllo, his sister who, in accordance with Inca tradition, became his wife to preserve the bloodline. Colonial portraits.

not do so because he feared that the Spaniards would immediately kill him. Pizarro demanded gold for the Sapa Inca's release. Atahualpa complied. He ordered treasure brought to Cajamarca. And Incas brought ornaments, dishes, sheets of gold from temples, and other objects that the Spaniards melted down and formed into gold bars.

Having kept his word, Atahualpa expected Pizarro to free him. Pizarro, however, believed that if he freed the Sapa Inca, Atahualpa would order his army to attack the Spaniards. In fact, some Spaniards believed Atahualpa had already done this secretly, although he had not. On the other hand, Pizarro concluded that he could not keep the Inca prisoner much longer. So the Spaniards charged him with plotting

Vicente de Valverde, Pizarro's chaplain and the first bishop of Cuzco.

their destruction. And after a brief trial, they convicted Atahualpa and condemned him to death.

Pedro Pizarro, a young cousin of Francisco who accompanied the expedition, told about the Sapa Inca's end.

Then Atahualpa wept, and he begged them not to kill him. There was not an Indian in the land who would stir without his command, he said. And he asked, what had they to fear, holding him prisoner? He said that if they were doing this thing for gold or silver, he would give them twice as much as he already had.

The Spaniards then took him out into the square at Cajamarca. They planned to strangle him. Atahualpa had told his Indians that if the Spaniards did not burn his body, he would return to them. His father the Sun would see to that.

Father Vicente de Valverde, a Spanish priest who was with Pizarro, preached to the Inca, asking him to become a Christian. He asked if they would burn him if he became a Christian. They told him no. He then said that if they would not burn him he would be baptized. And so Father Vicente baptized him and the Spaniards strangled him.

Pizarro and his men took Cuzco and captured many other Inca cities. Although Inca armies now fought the Spaniards, the invaders, thanks to their superior arms and their horses, conquered the entire empire within a decade. Added to the treasure that came from Mexico, Spanish riches in the New World now amounted to millions and millions of dollars.

Francisco Pizarro did not long enjoy either his position as governor and captain-general or his treasure. He quarreled with some of the men who had helped him conquer the empire of the Incas, and in June 1541 they killed him.

VOYAGES OF DISCOVERY AND EXPLORATION IN LATIN AMERICA

CORONADO
1540–42

DE SOTO
1539–42

NORTH AMERICA

Miss ss ippi R.

Rio Grande

PONCE DE LEÓN 1513

COLUMBUS 1492–93

FLORIDA

CABEZA DE VACA
1528–29; 1529–36

BAHAMA
ISLANDS

MEXICO

GULF OF MEXICO

Havana

San Salvador

CUBA

Santiago de Cuba

COLUMBUS 1493–96

Tenochtitlán

Tlaxcala

Veracruz

YUCATÁN
PENINSULA

HISPANIOLA

CORTÉS 1519
1524–26; 1535

HONDURAS

CARIBBEAN SEA

ATLANTIC OCEAN

BALBOA
1513

SPANISH MAIN

ISTHMUS OF
PANAMA

PIZARRO 1531–35

IS. ENCANTADAS
(GALÁPAGOS)

Equator

Quito

Amazon

Tumbes

Cajamarca

BRAZIL

PERU

Cuzco

SOUTH AMERICA

CABRAL 1500

PACIFIC OCEAN

L. Titicaca

A
N
D
E
S

M
O
U
N
T
A
I
N
S

500   1000   miles

0   500   1000   1500   kilometers

Hernán Cortés

The *Santa Maria*

An iguana

FALKLAND ISLANDS

Sea monster crushing a ship

Juan Ponce de León

Christopher Columbus

VICEREGAL RULE AND REVOLUTIONS

Laws for the Spanish colonies were made in Spain by the Royal and Supreme Council of the Indies, whose members were appointed by the king and were directly responsible to him. The king also chose viceroys and captains-general. Viceroys "stood in the place of the king." Although subject to Spanish government control, their power was considerable. And in the colonies they established and maintained the same centralized rule that prevailed in Spain.

Only men born in Spain received appointment as viceroys, as viceroys' advisers, or as high church officials. These men were known as *peninsulares*, a reference to the Iberian Peninsula formed by Spain and Portugal. *Criollos*, Spaniards born in the colonies, constituted a class just below peninsulares. Denied high government positions, criollos made up the majority of the colonial Catholic clergy and filled lesser jobs. Many became ranchers and mineowners. Many criollo families were wealthy enough to send sons to the universities Spain established in the Americas. (The first university in the Western Hemisphere was founded in Santo Domingo in 1538. Others soon opened in Mexico City and in Lima.) Below criollos were *mestizos*. These persons, born of mixed Indian-white parentage, made up the lower middle class of mine and plantation workers, artisans, and small merchants.

Indians formed the next class, ranking just above black slaves. Many Indians served in encomienda as laborers in gold and silver mines. Others worked under encomienda on large estates. A large number of Indians, particularly those who lived in remote mountain areas and in rain forests, continued their traditional tribal life without much reference to Europeans.

Laws enacted by the Council of the Indies governed Spanish treatment of Indians. Aroused by missionary reports of cruelty, the Council paid especial attention to encomienda. From time to time it tried to eliminate the system, but its efforts failed. Spanish colonists believed that gold, silver, and food production was impossible without Indian labor.

In the process of utilizing Indians, the Spaniards visited terrible hardship on them. No one knows how many Indians died as a direct result of war, hard labor, starvation, and sheer mental depression. Such diseases as smallpox, unknown to the Indians before whites arrived, took a particularly dreadful toll. One estimate placed the number lost at between twelve and thirteen million by 1541.

Black slavery also existed in the Spanish

Opposite: Simón Bolívar

colonies, especially on sugar plantations in the West Indies. Here colonists produced a crop for the world market, in the process absorbing thousands of blacks from Africa. And beginning in the seventeenth century, the Indies served as a way station from which blacks were retransported to the English colonies in North America.

THE ROLE OF THE CHURCH

A powerful influence in the Spanish New World, the Catholic church tolerated black slavery. On the other hand, the church generally served as the Indians' protector. It spoke out against their enslave-ment, concerning itself in particular with the enforcement of laws governing their treatment.

Missionary priests numbered conversions in the millions. To Indians, they preached the traditional Christian message: earthly life might be hard, but for the faithful there would be a reward in heaven. Indians accepted Christianity, but probably no group fully understood it or stopped worshipping their former gods.

Church officials constituted a separate group among the elite in Spanish America. As in Spain, the Catholic church was the official church in the colonies, supported by the government. The church operated missions, universities, and elementary schools. On the

The bishop of New Spain officiates at baptismal rites of Indians converted to Christianity. From an eighteenth century manuscript.

whole, however, education was limited to the privileged classes and did not reach the masses of the people.

The church baptized, married, and buried people, and it established and maintained cemeteries. It built cathedrals in every important city. It operated hospitals as well as schools. The church also owned banks. And it became an important landowner, holding Indians in encomienda. Interest on loans and rent from land and buildings afforded the church income to support itself and the various social services, such as education and health care, that it furnished. The traditional tithe—a person's contribution of one-tenth of his income to the church—was also a source of church revenues. The government collected the tithe and turned the money over to the church.

CONQUEST OR LIBERATION? INTERPRETING THE PAST

Historians have long disagreed in their evaluation of the Spanish experience in Latin America. On the one hand, there is the Black Legend. According to it, the Spaniards were cruel conquerors. They stole from Aztecs, Incas, and others. Through encomienda, they placed Indians in a state of slavery. The Spaniards' only motive was to exploit the New World's resources. In the process, through diseases they brought and by other means, they severely reduced an innocent Indian population. The Spaniards used Christianity as a means of achieving and ensuring Indian docility. The church did not do nearly as much as it could and should have done to make Indians' life easier. The church had as great a stake in exploiting Indians as Spanish colonists did.

Other historians present a different point of view. They do not deny that millions of Indians died. Nor do they deny that the Spaniards reaped great riches from their colonies.

However, they point out that the Aztecs, for example, were harsh rulers and that their Indian subjects were glad to be liberated from them. These historians praise the abolition of human sacrifice. The Inca empire also rested on subject peoples, and Spaniards freed them from Inca domination. Francisco Pizarro is generally considered a freebooter and a destroyer, but some historians see Cortés as a builder, one who laid firm foundations for a new society in Mexico. Historians who promote the so-called White Legend, or at least try to modify the Black, emphasize the protection that the Council of the Indies and the Catholic church afforded Indians. Without those influences, they contend, the Indians would have been much worse off. Some historians see Christianity as a beneficial force in other ways. They stress in particular the church's extension of medical care and hospitals, and the improved agricultural methods and breeding stock priests brought to the Americas.

The time of the Spanish conquest was a cruel age. Europe was periodically torn by war. Shortly after the conquest, groups broke away from the Catholic church to form Protestant churches. This, the Reformation or Protestant Rebellion, was followed by religious wars. These were frequently more bitter, cruel, and devastating than those fought only for territory. Thousands of Europeans died over the question of whether a nation would be Protestant or Catholic.

With respect to conquest, all Europeans shared certain beliefs. They believed that their civilization, based on technology and the desire for material wealth as well as on Christianity, was the best humans had ever created. Few Europeans appreciated any other culture. Further, they believed they had the right—in some cases the God-given right—to go wherever in the world they pleased and claim whatever land they chose. Europeans also had the ships and the armament. The idea that might makes right is age-old.

AN AGE OF EXPLOITATION

Historians might disagree on the effects of Spanish conquest. Most, however, agree that the Spanish American empire provided Spain with considerable wealth. In some Latin American cities the Spanish did establish some of the finer aspects of European civilization—drama, literary works, elegant architecture, and music. But their major goal was to exploit the continent's resources.

Spaniards were primarily a city people, but many established huge landed estates in Mexico and on the rolling grasslands of Venezuela and Argentina. And these estates produced not only wealth but also a subclass of men who tended herds. These men were known as *vaqueros* in Mexico, *llaneros* in Venezuela, and *gauchos* in Argentina. They were the cowboys of Latin America.

A rough, rude lot, fierce fighters in time of war, vaqueros, llaneros, and gauchos lived as extensions of their horses. To them their fleet and hardy animals were more valuable than anything else on earth, as this llanero poem indicates:

> Mi mujer y mi caballo
> Se me murieron a un tiempo;
> Que mujer, ní que demonio,
> Mi caballo es lo que siento.

> My wife and my horse
> Both died on me at once;
> To the devil with my wife,
> It's my horse I grieve for.

Sheep and cattle ranches were part of the frontier element that persisted in various areas

An Argentine gaucho, from an early photograph.

of Latin America during Spanish times. So were mining towns, the most famous of which was Potosí.

Potosí nestles in the Andes Mountains of Bolivia, about fourteen thousand feet above sea level. Today it holds about 65,000 people. Three centuries ago, more than twice that number lived there.

The Incas discovered the rich silver mines of Potosí early in the 1400s. According to legend, however, when the Sapa Inca began digging there a voice rang out: "Take no silver from these hills! It is destined for other owners."

Spaniards began to work the mines of Potosí with Indian labor around 1545. So fabulously rich were these mines that among Spaniards, *vale un Potosí*—worth a Potosí—was a phrase meaning "of infinite value."

Potosí became a boomtown on the most grand and lavish scale. It held some 160,000 persons by the middle of the seventeenth century. There was only one theater, but Potosí citizens in search of fun and relaxation could choose from among thirty-six gambling establishments. Residents celebrated the accession of Philip II to the Spanish throne in 1556 with a party that lasted twenty-four days and cost some eight million pesos.

Many newcomers were foreigners—that is, arrivals from France, England, and other countries—seeking fortunes. And the glory days of Potosí endured until the beginning of the nineteenth century, by which time most of the silver had been taken out. The population dropped to about eight thousand, later climbing to its present total.

If nothing else, Potosí symbolized exploitation. It stood as an example of European attitudes toward colonies and Indians. They existed to serve colonists and the mother country. Thousands of Indians died laboring underground in Potosí's mines. And the Portuguese who settled Brazil held ideas about overseas possessions identical to those of the Spaniards.

Portuguese ship captain Pedro Alvares Cabral, sailing for India and swinging southwest from Portugal to catch westerly winds, discovered Brazil in 1500. Formal Portuguese settlement began in 1530.

The king of Portugal portioned out huge sections of land, mainly to members of the Portuguese nobility. He granted them power to establish towns, distribute land to their followers, organize armies, collect taxes, and enslave Indians. After twenty years of loose rule under nobles, the king of Portugal appointed Thomé de Sousa the first governor-general of Brazil, bringing the entire area under closer royal control. Like the Spaniards, the Portuguese were Catholic, and Jesuit priests fanned out from such coastal settlements as Salvador da Bahia and São Paulo to establish missions among Indian tribes. By the end of the 1500s, some forty thousand Portuguese lived in Brazil in about twenty towns along the coast.

Most Portuguese settlers existed by farming and raising livestock. By the end of the sixteenth century, sugarcane was Brazil's most important cash crop. As in the West Indies, cane cultivation in Brazil rested on black slavery. By 1600 there were probably about fifteen thousand blacks laboring as slaves on Brazilian plantations.

The Portuguese also benefited from Brazil's mineral resources. Perhaps as much as a billion dollars worth of gold and some twenty to thirty million dollars worth of diamonds flowed from Brazilian mines.

Brazilian society was divided into classes, as was that of the Spanish colonies, but with one difference. The Portuguese were more inclined than the Spanish to ignore class and racial differences. Whites intermingled with blacks and Indians to a greater extent than in the Spanish areas, and there existed greater social mobility and racial tolerance.

By 1800 a large portion of the Americas had been held as Spanish and Portuguese colonies for almost three centuries. Then, within a quarter-century, nearly all of these holdings slipped from the control of Spain and Portugal.

BLACK SUCCESS

Black rebels in the French colony of Saint-Domingue, the western portion of the island known as Hispaniola or Santo Domingo, were the first people in Latin America to gain independence from Europeans. France had taken over Saint-Domingue in 1697, following war with Spain.

Under French rule Saint-Domingue became a land of sugarcane, coffee, cotton, and indigo, an ingredient for blue dye. Hundreds of thousands of blacks were imported from Africa to labor as slaves on plantations, and by the end of the eighteenth century, blacks far outnumbered whites. A census of 1788 showed only 28,000 whites against 405,000 slaves and 22,000 free blacks.

Saint-Domingue became a prosperous colony, and one possessing a complex social structure. At the top were *grands blancs,* wealthy white plantation owners and French government officials, the ruling class. Below them were *petits blancs,* or lesser whites, who were shopkeepers, workers in the crafts, and small farmers. Next came the *gens de couleur* (people of color), or mulattoes, of mixed black and white ancestry. Class lines were rigidly drawn. The races were segregated in churches and other public places. Grands blancs were determined to maintain their political and economic power, petits blancs desired more, and mulattoes wished to better their social and economic position. All this created a great deal of tension in the colony.

The French Revolution began in 1789. Frenchmen overthrew the monarchy, later ex-

A civil servant strolls to church, followed by his finely dressed family and household slaves in early nineteenth century Rio de Janeiro.

ccuting King Louis XVI and his queen, Marie Antoinette. They sought to establish a government based on human liberty and democracy.

Grands blancs in Saint-Domingue sent representatives to the National Assembly, the legislative body of the new French government. There they won the right to establish their own assembly in the colony. But during discussions about Saint-Domingue, the representatives inadvertently drew attention to slavery and the social conditions which existed there. A group called *Les Amis des Noirs,* friends of blacks, immediately began to spread antislavery propaganda in the colony.

In August 1791 slaves in the northern part of Saint-Domingue rebelled. As many as 100,000 blacks participated, killing whites and burning their homes, and destroying crops and sugar mills. Whites and mulattoes fought to put down the uprising, and in September 1792, 6,000 French troops arrived, along with commissioners to represent French authority in Saint-Domingue.

Britain and Spain were now at war with France, and both nations sent troops to try to wrest the colony from French control. Spanish forces withdrew in 1795, but the British stayed on until 1798, losing thousands of men in combat and to yellow fever. In the meantime, a black leader, Pierre Dominique Toussaint L'Ouverture, who had organized and trained a private army, steadily gained power.

Toussaint L'Ouverture, grandson of an African tribal chieftain, was born into slavery in 1743. His white master was different from most, however, in that he taught the young boy to read and write. In 1777 he freed Toussaint. An exceedingly able leader, Toussaint began to organize his army after news of the French Revolution reached Saint-Domingue.

The troops Toussaint directed burned plantations and killed many whites. They also captured arms and ammunition. By 1794 Toussaint had the northern portion of the colony under his control. This, plus the fact that Sonthonax, one of the French commissioners

who had arrived in 1792, sympathized with the black cause, brought about the abolition of slavery in Saint-Domingue, an act the French government confirmed in 1794. About ten thousand whites now left the island for the United States.

Pierre Dominique
Toussaint L'Ouverture

Having eliminated white power in the north, Toussaint turned his attention to defeating mulatto forces which had seized control in the south and west. He assigned this task to a lieutenant, Jean Jacques Dessalines, who did a thorough job, destroying plantations and ruining prime irrigation works in the process. By 1798 Toussaint had established himself as the principal leader in the colony. The following year, after he convinced the French government of his loyalty to France, he was named governor-general of Saint-Domingue.

Some whites who had left the colony began to return in the mid-1790s. A number of plantations were put back into operation. Blacks now worked for wages, not as slaves. In 1801 Toussaint issued a constitution, and during that same year his troops occupied Spanish Santo Domingo, giving the black leader mastery over the entire island.

Two years before, however, Napoleon Bonaparte had seized power in France, making himself head of the government. Napoleon planned to recreate a French empire in the Americas. To reestablish French power in Saint-Domingue, he sent an army of some twenty thousand men there, under the command of his brother-in-law, General Victor Leclerc. Toussaint was removed as head of the government.

Suspicions grew among Saint-Domingue Negroes that the French planned to restore slavery. Fearing that Toussaint might lead another rebellion, General Leclerc had him shipped to France. There he died in prison in April 1803.

Leadership of renewed rebellion fell to Jean Jacques Dessalines. Aided by yellow fever, which killed French soldiers by the tens of thousands, Dessalines defeated the French. What remained of the government army left Saint-Domingue late in 1803. On New Year's Day, 1804, Dessalines proclaimed the independence of Saint-Domingue and renamed it Haiti, an Indian word meaning mountainous.

Jean Jacques Dessalines harbored deep hatred for whites. After making himself emperor of Haiti, he invited whites who had left the island to come back. Those who did returned to their death. Dessalines himself was ambushed and killed by mulatto enemies in 1806.

Haiti remained independent, but thanks mainly to the destruction of plantations and irrigation works, it was an exceedingly poor country. It remained a land of dictatorships. One strong man after another came and went with dreary regularity following the death of Dessalines.

OTHER PATHS TO INDEPENDENCE

The forces behind revolutions in other parts of Latin America were not so clear and precise as in Haiti. Certainly the idea of the rights of man and the example of the American and French revolutions influenced the Latin American independence movement. So did the criollo desire for greater power and status. But although criollos may have wished to improve their lot, they were not an oppressed people. Spanish law severely restricted trade with countries other than Spain. Criollo merchants supported the independence movement because they hoped to gain freedom to trade with all nations. A number of mestizos, despite low social status, had acquired wealth, mainly through landowning. They wished to

exert greater influence on Latin American politics and society. Mestizos generally supported independence. No one, however, seemed to possess a strong desire to alter the social order drastically. Revolutionaries had destroyed the monarchy in France, attacked the nobility, and tried to trim the power of the Catholic church. But few if any of the men who spearheaded the Latin American independence movement had similar actions in mind.

The independence movement began following the French invasion of Spain in 1808. Napoleon Bonaparte conquered a portion of the country and replaced King Ferdinand VII with his own brother, Joseph Bonaparte. This presented colonial leaders who wished independence with an opportunity to try to overthrow Spanish domination. Simón Bolívar was one criollo who rose to leadership at this time.

SIMÓN BOLÍVAR, LIBERATOR

Diminutive Simón Bolívar—he stood only five feet two inches tall—was born the son of a wealthy landowning family in Venezuela in 1783. The Bolívars' roots in the New World wound back to forebears who had settled in Santo Domingo in the 1500s.

Both of Bolívar's parents died when he was a boy. Relatives raised him. At the age of sixteen he visited Spain, where he met Maria Teresa del Toro. Bolívar married her in 1802 when he was nineteen. Planning to lead the comfortable life of rich landowners, the Bolívars returned to Venezuela.

But in January 1803 Maria Teresa died. Bolívar, vowing never to remarry, returned to Europe in 1805. There he became acquainted with concepts about the rights of man that had led to the French Revolution. Bolívar took these ideas back to Venezuela with him in 1807, the year before Napoleon invaded Spain.

Simón Bolívar became a follower of Francisco de Miranda, who had led an unsuccessful uprising against the Spanish colonial government in 1806. In 1811 rebels tried once more, this time forming their own government. Regular Spanish armies loyal to the viceroy, however, experienced little difficulty in crushing the uprising. Leaving a vast fortune behind, Bolívar left for Colombia.

In Colombia, Bolívar formed and trained an army. In 1813 he invaded Venezuela. The following year the French were driven from Spain and Ferdinand VII regained the throne. Now full Spanish might could be brought to bear on rebellious activity in the colonies. Uprisings that had flared in Argentina, Peru, and elsewhere were put down, and Bolívar was forced to flee from Venezuela.

Not one to quit a chosen course, Bolívar once again gathered and trained an army. In 1817 he once more invaded Venezuela, this time successfully. Following the great rebel victory on the plains of Carabobo in 1821, Spanish forces were driven from Venezuela. Bolívar's final battle against the Spanish occurred in Peru in 1824. Rebel leaders formed the nation of Gran Colombia, eventually consisting of present-day Venezuela, Ecuador, Colombia, and Panama. Simón Bolívar, hailed as *El Libertador* in Peru, became Gran Colombia's first president.

Bolívar supported the establishment of large political units like Gran Colombia and strong central governments. Other leaders, however, did not agree. Numerous local strong men sprang up throughout Gran Colombia. And on more than one occasion local chieftains raised the standard of rebellion against Bolívar's government. In September 1828 his enemies tried to assassinate him. By this time, although only forty-five years old, Bolívar was a sick and worn-out man, and a bitter one. In a conversation with a French doctor he asked:

"Doctor, what did you come to this country to find?"

"Liberty," the doctor replied.

"Have you found it?"

"Yes, general," the doctor replied.

"Then you are more fortunate than I am," said Bolívar. "Go back to your fair France, where the tricolor [the French flag] is still flying. Here in this country, no one can live. Too many crooks, *canallas*."

Disillusioned about his life work, Bolívar said, "We who have struggled for the independence of America have plowed the sea."

Simón Bolívar died December 17, 1830. A week before, he had made his last speech as president, in which he said: "Colombians, my latest wish is for the happiness of our country. If my death can help put an end to party strife and uphold the Union, I shall go down to the grave in peace." That wish was not fulfilled. The same year Bolívar died, Ecuador and Venezuela withdrew from Gran Colombia and declared themselves independent nations.

Elsewhere in South America, Argentina gained independence from Spain under the leadership of José de San Martín. San Martín then led his army across the Andes, skillfully hiding from the Spanish. Along with Bernardo O'Higgins, son of an Irish immigrant, San Martín attacked the Spanish in Chile, finally making that country independent. San Martín then led forces against the Spanish in Peru, helping to achieve that nation's independence. Paraguay became a nation in the early 1820s. And in 1825 a Bolívar lieutenant, Antonio José de Sucre, freed Bolivia —named after El Libertador—from Spanish rule.

Uruguay gained independence not from Spain but from Brazil. In 1825 Juan Lavalleja, aided by Argentina, led a revolt against Brazilian domination. This action developed into a three-year war between Argentina and Brazil, which ended with the establishment of the Republic of Uruguay.

Brazil itself became independent without war. Following France's invasion of his country in 1807, the prince regent of Portugal,

John, fled to Brazil. Crowned king in 1816, John VI was forced to return home in 1821 when a revolt broke out in Lisbon. He left his son Pedro to rule the colony. Caught up in the independence movement, Brazilians demanded freedom from Portuguese control. So in 1822 Pedro declared Brazil a sovereign nation and had himself crowned as king. Under Pedro and his son Pedro II, Brazil remained a monarchy until 1889.

REBEL PRIESTS

In Haiti, black slaves led the independence movement. In South America it was led by criollos. In Mexico, a Roman Catholic priest, Miguel Hidalgo y Costilla, led the first attempt to gain independence from Spain.

Hidalgo's first objective was to destroy encomienda. At the same time, he wanted his people to be free from Spanish rule.

Indians and mestizos who listened to Hidalgo preach grasped little of what he said about independence and the rights of man. But they did understand encomienda. And they rallied behind Hidalgo to throw the system off.

On September 15, 1810, Hidalgo led an army of nearly sixty thousand against the city of Guanajuato in northern Mexico. When the Spanish there refused to surrender, Hidalgo and his men attacked. Armed only with bows and arrows, stones, *machetes* (large heavy knives for cutting brush), and burning torches, they nevertheless took the city. Thousands of lives on both sides were lost.

Hidalgo's success thoroughly alarmed Mexico's colonial government and leaders of the Mexican church. The church dismissed Hidalgo from the priesthood. The government organized an army against Hidalgo's forces, now numbering about eighty thousand men.

Hidalgo moved south toward Mexico City, fighting several bloody battles along the way. But Hidalgo began to lose control over his men. Soon they were killing all the Europeans they could find, women and children as well as men. Thousands perished in what had become class warfare.

Early in 1811, the Spanish captured Hidalgo and executed him.

This did not end the Mexican independence movement. Another priest, José María Morelos, a mestizo, now took command. Disciplining his troops and keeping them under firm control, he also organized a government. In 1814 Morelos declared Mexico independent and had a constitution written. The document authorized the new government to take land and other possessions from peninsulares and other wealthy people and distribute them to the poor.

Morelos met the same fate as Hidalgo. In December 1815 the Spaniards captured him and placed him before a firing squad.

After several more years of armed conflict, independence finally came to Mexico under a criollo and former officer in the Spanish army, Agustín de Iturbide. Appointed by the viceroy to erase revolutionary activity in Mexico, Iturbide secretly befriended rebel leaders who moved to the top following Morelos's execution. Conservatives and church leaders who wished to continue their favored status in Mexico supported Iturbide too. Eventually he assumed command. A mutiny of Spanish soldiers in Mexico City in July 1821 opened that city to Iturbide's forces. Mexico became independent and in 1822 Iturbide made himself emperor, Agustín I.

Central America declared its independence from Spain in the early 1820s. The nations of Honduras, Guatemala, El Salvador, Costa Rica, and Nicaragua were later formed in the area.

COLONIAL POWERS IN LATIN AMERICA IN 1784

San Francisco

VICEROYALTY
OF
NEW SPAIN

Santa Fe

NORTH AMERICA

Rio Grande

• Guadalajara

St. Augustine •

New Orleans •

FLORIDA

GULF OF MEXICO

Havana •

Mexico City •

CUBA

Port au Prince •

Santo Domingo

JAMAICA

ATLANTIC OCEAN

Guatemala City •

SAINT-DOMINGUE   HISPANIOLA   PUERTO
RICO

CARIBBEAN SEA

Santa Marta •

Caracas •

VICEROYALTY
OF
NEW GRANADA

Panama City •

Cayenne •

GUIANA

Bogotá •

IS. ENCANTADAS
(GALÁPAGOS)

Equator

• Quito

Manaus •

Pará •

PACIFIC OCEAN

Lima •

VICEROYALTY
OF
BRAZIL

Salvador da Bahia •

Cuzco •

• La Paz

• Potosí

VICEROYALTY
OF
PERU

Rio de Janeiro •

São Paulo •

VICEROYALTY
OF
LA PLATA

Santiago •

Santa Fe •

SOUTH AMERICA

Buenos Aires •

Montevideo •

EUROPEAN COLONIES

New Spain
New Granada   Spain
Peru
La Plata

Portugal

France

Great Britain

Disputed Territory

Claimed but not
settled by Spain

0   500   1000 miles

0   500   1000   1500 kilometers

IS. MALVINAS
(FALKLANDS)

Unit 2
FROM INDEPENDENCE TO THE PRESENT

Independence changed the Latin American social structure in only one way. Criollos instead of peninsulares were now the upper class. As before, mestizos ranked below criollos, and Indians below mestizos. Black slaves stayed at the bottom.

Despite the efforts of Bolívar and some others to prevent it, Latin America with its sixteen million inhabitants split into several nations shortly after independence. And each nation faced similar problems.

What form of government should be established? Some leaders favored monarchy. Others supported an oligarchy, rule by a select few. Still others believed in rule by a strong man. Few people of any prominence advocated representative democracy.

The Roman Catholic church had been a powerful institution during colonial times. It was closely allied with government. What should the relationship between church and state be now?

What should be done for or about the Indian population that had formerly served in encomienda? Should land be distributed to landless peasants? What about slavery?

These were the most important of the numerous problems facing new Latin American nations. Some were solved. Others remain unsolved today. Still others, at least in the beginning, were ignored.

Opposite: The baroque doorway of a colonial church in Cochabamba, Bolivia. The small figures over the pillars mark the work of Indian craftsmen.

POLITICAL TURMOIL

On the whole, the Latin American record concerning slavery was good. The Saint-Domingue constitution of 1801 abolished the institution there. Slaves were emancipated in Argentina in 1812, in Chile in 1823, in Bolivia three years later. Mexico abolished slavery in 1829. Except for Brazil, slavery ceased to exist in Latin America after the 1850s. The institution persisted in Brazil until 1888.

The abolition of slavery was a humanitarian step. But at the same time, in most areas the slave population was small. Indians and mestizos formed an ample labor supply. European immigration eventually swelled the labor force in Brazil, and this had much to do with slavery's end there.

Little was done to improve the lot of Indians. They remained for the most part an exploited people.

The Roman Catholic church had enjoyed a privileged position during colonial times. Church officials expected to maintain control over vast landholdings, and over banks, schools, and other institutions. New governments made Catholicism the official religion and cooperated with the church to keep Protestantism out of Latin America. This effort was not entirely successful. Protestantism, however, never became a major force in any Latin American country. The masses of the people remained Catholic. Among Indians, religion continued a mixture of Catholicism and age-old beliefs and practices.

BASES OF POWER: THE CAUDILLO

The patterns of power and class structure that had developed during three centuries of Spanish rule deeply influenced the governments that evolved in Latin America. Viceroys had exercised absolute authority. The people had enjoyed no experience with democracy or representative government. Among the masses of the people, the idea of elections was unknown. At the same time, Latin Americans possessed a Spanish heritage of fierce individualism. They did not think of government in the abstract, but tended to attach themselves to a leader, local or national, and give him personal support. And, just as Latin America split into several nations, so did groups within nations divide into factions, many of them all too ready to settle issues with guns and machetes.

Some independence leaders appear to have held democracy and representative government as a long range ideal. Most, however, preferred a monarchy or an oligarchy. They

Opposite: Mexicans of different social classes enjoy an outing beside the Guanajuato River. A painting from about 1850.

argued that the people's low level of literacy and total lack of experience with democratic institutions justified such attitudes. Still, following the lead of the United States, all Latin American countries during the nineteenth century established constitutions providing for republican governments. The documents called for a judicial system, a president, and elected representatives to make laws. However, as one historian has remarked, "No other part of the world had more constitutions or observed them less." Strong man rule became the norm. It became common procedure for a president to suspend or set aside a constitution and rule dictatorially. Elections were held frequently. But the results were not always accepted. On numerous occasions, defeated candidates simply substituted bullets for ballots to gain offices elections denied them.

Latin Americans tended to take politics personally and, in many instances, passionately. An opponent was frequently viewed not simply as a rival for political office but as an enemy. And in the rough-and-tumble political arena of the nineteenth century, especially, it was common for winners to have losers shot.

Generally speaking, the century following independence marked the age of the *caudillo*, the strong man or military dictator. This was the case on both local and national levels. To become a caudillo, a man needed first of all to possess *macho*—aggressive masculinity. He had to know how to manipulate and dominate others. And he had to be ruthless in his quest for power and in the way he exercised it. Possessing these qualities, a man might lead armed followers to insure his election, to succeed in a rebellion, or to pull off a *golpe de estado*—a sudden and frequently bloodless seizure of power. Once in power, however, a caudillo had to keep his followers satisfied. He had to parcel out the spoils he had won. And he had to be ever watchful. Caudillismo was a fiercely competitive game.

Most caudillos were army officers. Some were simply bandits who stole and gunned their way to power. A few were civilians able to win army backing. Some were white, some were Indian or black. Most were mestizos. Some were sober, upright individuals. Others were corrupt and sensual, with a liking for strong drink and wild living. Some were bitterly anti-Catholic. Others were piously religious. Some caudillos developed constructive programs that benefited their countries. Others had no programs at all, save to enrich themselves and their followers at public expense.

BASES OF POWER: THE CHURCH

Throughout the colonial period, the Catholic church was the established, or official, church of Latin America. Governments under the viceroys supported the Catholic church, and the church, in turn, supported the governments. As the official religious institution, the church served two roles. One was spiritual. The other was temporal—that is, earthly.

In fulfilling the church's spiritual role, priests baptized, married, and buried people, heard confessions, and celebrated Mass. They organized fiestas and processions on saints' days and on such special days as Christmas and Easter.

On the temporal side, the church owned land and buildings. Mestizo and Indian peasants worked the land on either a rental or a share-cropping basis. Income from farms and from buildings in cities and contributions from individual members provided the church with resources to carry out other temporal functions. These included the building and operation of hospitals and such charitable activities as aiding the poor, the orphaned, and the widowed.

The Catholic church also played an important role in the education of the people, and here the spiritual and temporal functions overlapped. Children attending church-supported schools learned to read and write. At the same time, they received instruction in the Catholic faith.

Few Latin Americans had any quarrel with the church over its spiritual role. Whether they attended Mass regularly or not, most Latin Americans were Catholics, and they wished to be married and buried in the church and have their children baptized in it. After the independence movement and into the nineteenth and twentieth centuries, however, a growing number of people came to oppose the church's active participation in politics and its temporal role in general.

Critics accused the church of using its vast resources to support conservative and reactionary groups and to resist attempts to improve the lives of the people. They agreed that the church provided valuable social services, such as health care and charity, but they maintained that the church simply manipulated Indian and mestizo peasants, in effect keeping them in encomienda. Critics further contended that the main objective of church schools was not to teach children to read and write or even to dispense religious education. Rather, it was to produce citizens who would follow the direction of the church on every issue in which the church had an interest.

One of the greatest controversies grew out of the church's role as a landholder. Land was the most important form of wealth in Latin America. Most of it was owned either by criollos or by the Catholic church. Upon achieving independence, every country developed two political groups: the conservatives and the liberals. Liberals and conservatives invariably clashed over state policies regarding landownership.

Most liberals were mestizos. They did not wish to destroy the Latin American class system. They did, however, wish to rise in it.

They would do so only by acquiring land. Because liberals saw nothing wrong with private ownership of wealth, they did not advocate taking land from criollos. Consequently, they chose to sell at least a portion of its land to individuals, including themselves, the mestizos.

Some liberals went further. They wanted the government to seize church lands and distribute them to peasants, by outright gift if necessary. Peasants were compelled to work for others, to scratch out an existence without hope of ever improving their lives. Being given some land of their own would enable them to break the cycle.

There were other issues over which liberals and conservatives fought. Liberals wished a complete separation of church and state. Conservatives did not. Liberals wanted government to be responsible for education and other social services. Conservatives wanted to leave these duties in the hands of the church.

Understandably, the church opposed any plan to take away its land. The leaders of the Catholic church believed that without the rent from its lands, the church would be unable to carry out many of its functions, especially the social services it performed. Furthermore, church officials viewed any attempt to exclude the church from its traditional functions—such as education—as a threat to both its spiritual and temporal positions. Therefore, to counter the threats of the liberals the church sided with the conservatives.

The question of loyalty also became a problem. Liberals feared that the church might use its schools to promote greater loyalty to itself rather than to the nation and its government. They also feared that the church might use social services in the same way.

A great deal was at stake in these church-related controversies. Unfortunately, in the absence of a tradition of political give-and-take, conservatives and liberals frequently

Carved statuary and stuccowork, dazzling with gold and brilliant color, seem to cover every inch of the church of Santa María de Tonantzintla, near Cholula, Mexico.

resorted to armed force to win their points concerning the church, land distribution, and other issues. As a result, the army became an important element in Latin American politics. To win control of the army was to control the government. This remains a fact of life in Latin America politics today.

BASES OF POWER: LATIFUNDIA

As conservatives, criollo landowners tended to ally themselves with the church. It was easy for them to see that if a government could take land from one source, it could take it from another.

For individual landowning families, what had been encomienda during colonial times became *latifundia* following independence. Latifundia referred to large landholdings and the control of peasants who worked them. In Mexico wealthy landowners were known as *hacendados*, ruling over ranches called *haciendas*. In some other parts of Latin America they were known as *estancieros* and their holdings as *estancias*.

Hacendados and estancieros used peasants to raise crops and care for cattle and sheep. They furnished peasants with food, clothing, and shelter. And through overseers and foremen they kept peasants under tight control. Estate owners themselves usually resided most of the time in cities, visiting their holdings only now and then.

Writing in the late 1960s, Latin American scholar Victor Alba pointed out that almost 88 percent of the cultivated land in Latin America consisted of holdings of 2,500 acres or more—almost one-fourth of it huge holdings of 250,000 acres or larger. The remaining 12 percent of land under cultivation consisted of farms of 250 acres or less. Yet more than 90 percent of Latin American farms were this size. Alba had this to say about latifundia:

> The typical latifundist lives in the large cities or abroad (in the late nineteenth century, Paris was the fashionable city) and many times has not even visited the lands from which he derives his income. He is not interested in modernizing his plantation or in increasing its yield, since this is already sufficient to permit him to live royally and even to invest abroad. He prefers to buy more land rather than increase the output of the land he already has. Only 2.6 percent of the arable surface of Brazil is under cultivation. Of Venezuela's 175 million arable acres, only 1.8 million acres are under cultivation. Only 65 million of the 215 million acres suitable for agriculture in Argentina are being utilized.

Latifundism has also tended to foster one-

Detail of an arch in the eighteenth century Loreto Chapel at Tepotzotlán, Mexico.

crop farming, which is simpler and more profitable. This has exposed the country's economy to the price fluctuations of raw materials on the world market and has limited cultivation of foodstuffs to the lands near the cities and to small individual lots. The result is an unbalanced diet, a high percentage of family expenditure for food, and virtually nonexistent savings for the common people. By leaving many peasants with very small farms, it has also encouraged minifundism [the division of land into small, unproductive plots]. . . . Finally, latifundism has deprived the countries of captial, and thus obliged them to accept foreign capital in order to create industries and public services.

Latifundism's human toll, according to Alba, has been tremendous. It has, he noted,

> kept the great rural masses—the majority of the population—on the fringes of the national cultural, economic, and political

life. This is the result of the systems of servitude . . . into which the landholding Creoles [criollos] transformed what survived of the customs of the encomienda. In some countries, these systems of servitude have been kept alive by tradition. In others (Ecuador, and Bolivia before 1952), they have even been sanctioned by law.

These systems have prevailed in countries with a large Indian population. But they have also existed in other countries, disguised as tenant farming. Latin American sharecropping often includes furnishing labor as part of the rental, the rest of which is paid by a percentage of the harvest. In this way, the tenant farmer is obliged to work the latifundist's lands, just as in the Middle Ages he would have had to work on the lands of his lord. It is not unusual, when a latifundio is sold, for the peasants who work on it, and their cattle, to be transferred also. There are places in which the peasant's second name is that of the landowner.

The phenomenon of latifundism points up starkly the fact that in Latin America following independence there was no middle class to speak of. The majority of the people were divided into a huge mass—the poor and the landless—and a tiny, controlling group—the landed and the rich.

As part of his study of a small town in Colombia, anthropologist Miles Richardson brought the plight of the landless Latin American down to the personal level:

Conceived in the hostility between the hacendado and the Indian was a child ordained for despair. The child was the landless mestizo. Having adopted the language and values of the hacendado, the mestizo could not and would not rest in the uneasy comfort of an Indian pueblo. Unable to accumulate even a fraction of the capital

necessary to purchase life-supporting land, the rural mestizo took the only route opened to him. He became a tenant of the hacendado. Such a man in the 1960s is Asael Guachabés, worker on the hacienda, Bomboná.

From the hacendado Asael receives about 7 acres of land. On this land he has built his shack and cultivates coffee, plantains [a variety of banana plant], oranges, manioc [root plant used for making flour], and a little tobacco. From Asael the hacendado receives 117 days of labor plus 25 pesos in cash (a little more than $2.50. The hacendado grades his workers according to their ability, and Asael was a first-class worker. He had a serious accident and not only did he lose two years of work, but when he returned, his diminished productivity placed him in the second category. His debt to the hacendado for the use of the land, sharply increased by the two years lost, has reached the point that, at Asael's present capacity, he will have to work fifteen years simply to get even. If he is to get out of debt before he dies, his only hope is his eldest son. However, the son, having observed the luck of his father, is going to take his chances, risky as they are, with the city.

Asael ponders his fate. "I was born here, my parents and my grandparents lived here. What can we do? What will happen will be what God wants." But as he thinks of what God wants, he sings to himself this refrain, "Now my dogs are dead. Now only my lonely shack remains. Tomorrow I, myself, will die, so that it may be finished."

BASES OF POWER: FOREIGNERS

A third element entered the power picture in Latin America shortly after independence. This was investment by companies from the United States and Europe. Investments ranged from banana and coffee plantations in Central America to rubber plantations in Brazil. They included oil wells and refineries in Mexico and Venezuela and copper mines in Chile.

Foreign investors, like church officials and large landowners, were conservative. They—and their governments—tended to support Latin American governments that promised maximum protection to their holdings. Foreign investors on the whole lined up with the Latin American elite to oppose economic and social change. Almost invariably they considered such change a threat to their interests. And almost invariably they were right.

Foreign-owned companies in Latin America provided jobs. In many instances they offered workers adequate housing, health care, and schooling. But liberals chafed under what they considered foreign domination of their countries. They noted that most of the profits that foreign companies earned flowed out of Latin America. In addition, the companies as a rule paid only low taxes. Liberals contended that Latin Americans themselves should exploit and receive maximum benefits from their countries' resources.

One problem, of course, was the attitude of wealthy Latin Americans toward land. They usually preferred to invest in more land, not in industry. Land, which could not be destroyed or carried away, seemed to them a more stable investment. Consequently there was little native capital available to promote manufacturing. It had to come from outside.

Most foreign investment was in industries such as mining and plantation farming that were geared toward foreign markets. In such industries many jobs could be performed by cheap, unskilled labor. This kept labor costs low. More important perhaps, the resources being exploited—such as copper and bananas—were abundant. Investment costs were lower and profits could be realized more quickly than in manufacturing. Foreign companies engaged in manufacturing consumer products needed export markets, and they preferred to sell their goods to Latin American countries, rather than invest in factories to produce such goods there.

Accordingly, when world prices for such Latin American products as copper and coffee were high, there were jobs aplenty. Many people benefited. But when prices fell, many were immediately out of work. There were no alternative jobs for them, as there are in a diversified economy where one finds many kinds of industries.

In no country, perhaps, were the power elements characterizing much of Latin American history more sharply defined than in Mexico. There an intense power struggle involving caudillos, the church, the state, hacendados, and foreign investors continued off and on for more than a century.

MEXICO, GROWTH PANGS OF A NATION

Chapter 6

Mexico became independent in 1821 and in June of the following year Colonel Agustín de Iturbide, who had won the final battles for freedom from Spain, proclaimed himself Emperor Agustín I. Agustín I did not last long. In December 1822 a disgruntled army officer named Antonio López de Santa Anna issued a *pronunciamiento* —a proclamation of rebellion—against him and overthrew the emperor. Banished from Mexico, Iturbide lacked the wisdom to stay out. Returning in July 1824, he faced a firing squad.

A great organizer able to attract many followers, Santa Anna was essentially a fortune hunter and a glory hound. He would play an important and on the whole a damaging role in Mexican affairs for many years.

During the same year they executed Iturbide, Mexican political leaders wrote a constitution. The document provided for a congress, a president, and a federal form of government. The 1824 constitution placed considerable power in the states, which were based in part on the old Spanish administrative districts under the viceroy. Each state had its own assembly and governor.

Elected president in 1824, Guadalupe Victoria served out his full term of four years. This example was not followed, however. Its central government weak, its people without political experience, Mexico was in for decades of political turmoil.

In 1829 King Ferdinand VII attempted to reestablish Spanish control over Mexico by landing an invasion force. This ill-advised move proved unsuccessful. Santa Anna led a Mexican army against the Spanish force and defeated it. Santa Anna became a national hero, and for a time he ruled as dictator.

The Mexico over which Santa Anna ruled was almost twice the size it is today. Texas, California, New Mexico, Arizona, Nevada, Utah, and part of Colorado then belonged to Mexico.

Beginning in the 1820s, the Mexican government encouraged United States citizens to immigrate to Texas by selling them land cheaply. The area was practically uninhabited save for scattered Indian tribes. By 1835, about thirty thousand English-speaking North Americans lived in Texas. And they grew impatient. They disliked Mexican political instability—hardly a year passed without a pronunciamiento of some degree of seriousness. Texans did not care to pay taxes to the Mexican government. They did not wish to become Catholics or learn Spanish. Most of all, perhaps, Texans wanted their own government under loose, if any, Mexican control.

Opposite: Mexican forces drive out the French at Puebla, May 5, 1862. Young Porfirio Díaz leads the army from a rearing stallion, center. A reinforced French army took the city the following year.

In 1835 Texans declared themselves independent of Mexico. Santa Anna marched an army north to subdue the rebels. Surrounding about 150 Texans holed up in the Alamo, a mission outside San Antonio, Santa Anna's army wiped them out. Later, when his army captured 300 Texans near the settlement of Goliad, the general had them shot.

Under Sam Houston, the Texans regrouped and surprised Santa Anna at San Jacinto. There the dictator's army was routed. He agreed to Texan independence, but later refused to honor the agreement.

Santa Anna had lost Texas. Later he lost more of Mexico.

In 1845 the United States admitted Texas as a state. A boundary dispute followed. Mexico claimed the Nueces River as the southern Texas boundary. The United States insisted that it should be the Rio Grande, farther south. In 1846 United States President James K. Polk ordered forces into the disputed territory. Mexican soldiers fired on them, killing eleven. The two nations were now at war. Deciding which side began the war depends a great deal on how one defines aggression.

The conflict lasted two years. Although Mexican soldiers fought fiercely and with great valor, they were on the whole poorly led. Owing to dissatisfaction with the Mexican government, there was little public support for the war. Mexicans were no more united in war than they were in peace.

The war ended in 1848 with Mexico defeated and forced to give up not only Texas, but California and what is now the Southwest as well. This meant a loss of about half of Mexico's territory. For this large but lightly populated area the United States paid Mexico the sum of fifteen million dollars. Later Santa Anna sold part of Arizona to the United States for ten million dollars. Although Mexico had held little real control over these territories, their loss was keenly resented by Mexicans.

LIBERAL LAWS AND A NEW CONSTITUTION

Antonio López de Santa Anna had been in and out of Mexican politics for several years. He left public life for the last time in 1855 and died forgotten twenty-one years later.

By the mid-1850s a new generation, most of them liberals, was in control. Blaming their country's problems on the Catholic church, they enacted the law known as *Ley Lerdo*. Ley Lerdo forced the church to sell land that was not being used for religious purposes. The law also made towns and Indian villages give up their communal holdings. All land was to become the property of individuals. The government hoped to create a new class of small landholders. Its leaders also expected to collect taxes on these land sales.

But the law didn't work out the way liberals had expected. For one thing, Indians and other peasants lacked the money to buy land. Many preferred the traditional system of communal ownership. In addition, revenues from church land had been paying for a number of social services that the government could not afford to provide for the people.

Many Catholics refused to bid on church lands when the church threatened to excommunicate them if they did so. As a result, much of the church land as well as the Indian land released for sale went to speculators.

In 1857 liberals wrote a new constitution that further angered conservatives and church leaders. Provisions of this constitution called for freedom of speech and of the press. The constitution also abolished special courts that had been maintained by the church and by the military. Both the church and the army opposed the new constitution, and civil war followed from 1858 to the beginning of 1861. And out of the conflict a leader emerged, a Zapotec Indian lawyer named Benito Juárez.

Born to a poor family in the state of Oaxaca in 1806, orphaned at age three, Benito Juárez was the servant of a clergyman who helped him to begin studies for the priesthood. Later Juárez switched to law. He rose from small-town lawyer to governor of Oaxaca, and then to important posts in the national government. A strong believer in the rule of law and liberal principles, Juárez was always ready to listen to Indian delegations. He often defended Indians in court when they had been tricked out of their land and water rights. He tried to better the lot of the Indian masses by working for a system of free public schools. Although Juárez considered the Catholic church corrupt and oppressive, he did not wish to destroy it. But he did believe that it possessed too much power.

A great deal of legend and controversy surrounds the man. To many Mexicans Juárez became and remains a great national hero. To others, he was a "bandit," an "atheist," and a "murderer." He was a species of caudillo, especially among his Indian followers.

WAR OF THE REFORM

The furor over the 1857 constitution erupted into civil war known as the Three Years' War or the War of the Reform.

The old order, representing the conservatives and the Catholic church, controlled Mexico City. Juárez, who succeeded to the presidency when President Ignacio Comonfort went into exile, set up a liberal government away from the capital. Juárez's government issued severe decrees aimed at the Catholic church, seizing their lands and buildings.

The War of the Reform came to a close with liberal victory. Benito Juárez now became president in fact as well as in law. But his country was in ruins. Farm production was almost nonexistent. Mines had been neglected. The treasury was empty and the army went unpaid. The people were far from united.

FOREIGN INTERVENTION

Following the war, Britain, Spain, and France brought claims against the Juárez government for war losses and other debts, a total of eighty million pesos. When Juárez decided that the government must suspend payment on its foreign debt for two years, the European nations used this excuse to intervene. They intended to take over Mexican ports to obtain duties, or taxes, paid on imported goods. When France indicated it had more ambitious plans than recovering its debts, England and Spain withdrew.

France's ruler at the time was Napoleon III, nephew of Napoleon Bonaparte. Napoleon III possessed his uncle's vision of France's greatness. Seeing an opportunity to gain an empire in North America, Napoleon III ordered troops to Mexico. Cheered by conservatives, the French ruler installed Archduke Maximilian of Austria as emperor of Mexico.

The French never succeeded in subduing more than a fraction of Mexico. Juárez fled the capital but his armies and guerrilla bands fought the French continually. Finally, owing partly to urging by the United States, which did not relish the idea of a European power in control of land so close to home, Napoleon III withdrew his support from Maximilian. Juárez's forces captured Maximilian and in 1867 Juárez had the former emperor shot.

Benito Juárez began to rebuild his country and he tried to unite it. Enjoying considerable popular support, especially among the lower classes, he had some success, until 1871. In that year Juárez ran for the presidency against two other candidates. No one received a majority of votes and the Mexican congress awarded the office to Juárez. A defeated candidate, army officer Porfirio Díaz, a mestizo, promptly charged fraud. Díaz's forces met defeat, but in July 1872 Juárez died. After four years of chaos, Porfirio Díaz took over in 1876. Díaz would hold power as president or president-maker for thirty-five years.

A TIME OF PEACE

As dictator, Díaz brought peace to Mexico and to a large extent modernized the country. Through bribery and brute force and by parceling out political favors, he kept local caudillos quiet. He kept the army loyal by paying his generals well and moving them periodically from post to post to prevent them from forming a local following. Those parts of the 1857 constitution that provided for freedom of speech and of the press were ignored. Whenever necessary, critics of the government were either jailed or shot. Traditional church privileges respecting tithing, landholding, and education went undisturbed. Díaz maintained order in the provinces by creating the *guardias rurales,* a ruthless, well-paid national police force. The rurales, some people said, were simply trigger-happy ruffians unin-terested in justice. Frequently those taken by the rurales were dealt with according to the *ley fuga*—the law of flight. They were killed "while attempting to escape," but they were not always shot in the back. The rurales did keep the peace, however, and many hacendados were satisfied with Díaz for that reason.

The dictator surrounded himself with able advisors and government officials known as the *científicos,* or scientists. They saw to it that taxes were collected and that Mexican credit with foreign nations remained sound. Díaz also encouraged foreign investment. Foreign companies built railroads and opened silver, gold, lead, and zinc mines. They purchased land to grow coffee and bananas and invested in and built electric lighting systems and streetcar lines in cities. The government kept taxes on foreign companies low, and most of the profits were taken out of Mexico.

Pancho Villa occupying the presidential chair in 1914 after revolutionary forces seized Mexico City. Beside Villa is Emiliano Zapata, his high-crowned sombrero resting on his knee.

A benevolent despot, though not without his ruthless side, Díaz brought peace and a measure of prosperity to Mexico. Little of the prosperity filtered down to the masses, however; they remained as poor and illiterate as ever. And the price of peace and prosperity was rather high. It included a congress without power—Díaz referred to its members as "my band of tame horses." The price also included regular elections without meaning, the suppression of free speech and press, and eventual control by Díaz's personal friends and foreigners of about a fifth of Mexico's total acreage. Díaz also allowed individuals to buy Indian communal land, under provisions of the Ley Lerdo. By 1910 hardly a tenth of Mexico's Indian communities possessed any land at all. Thousands of Yaqui Indians objected to losing their land. The rurales and the army rounded them up and shipped them off to work as slaves on plantations. Hacendados, foreign investors, and the church honored the Díaz regime. A good many Mexicans did not.

A TIME OF WAR

But dictators, like all mortals, grow old. Eighty years old in 1910, Díaz faced his first real opposition. It began with a book.

The book, *La Sucesión Presidencial en 1910* (The Presidential Succession in 1910), had been published in 1908. Written by Francisco Madero, mild and kindly but weak-willed son of a wealthy landowner, it discussed the question of who might succeed Díaz in office. Madero seems to have been interested mainly in a free and open vice-presidential election. He hoped, perhaps, to run successfully for the office and place himself in line for the presidency. Don Porfirio, after all, could not live forever.

Díaz paid little attention to the book. He did nothing to prevent Madero from making speeches about free elections until he noticed that his opponent was attracting large crowds. Then Díaz had Madero clapped in jail.

Díaz and his chosen vice-presidential candidate easily won election in 1910. Out of jail, Madero left Mexico for the United States. Then a peasant in the north named Doroteo Arango—better known as Pancho Villa—began a revolt on Madero's behalf. So did Emiliano Zapata, an Indian tenant farmer with many faithful followers. Now events began to snowball. After Madero returned to Mexico, caudillos arose in several provinces and Díaz was forced to resign. He retired to France, where he died four years later.

Madero won election as president in October 1911. But as a national leader, he left much to be desired. He lacked macho. He neither looked nor acted the part of the caudillo. Hordes of greedy, landholding relatives surrounded him. His brother Gustavo really ran the government. Madero demonstrated singularly poor judgment when he chose to rely for armed support on a crude, alcoholic, would-be caudillo named Victoriano Huerta, who had his personal army. In 1913 Huerta rebelled against Madero and took over the government. Huerta had Madero shot and proclaimed himself president.

Conservatives had considered Madero too liberal. They looked upon Huerta as Mexico's savior, foreseeing a return to the golden days of Díaz. This too was a mistake. For some sixteen months, spending more time in saloons than in the presidential palace, Huerta did his best to ruin his country, aided by his gang of armed thugs.

At first foreign interests supported Huerta. But the United States finally turned against him and helped to arm Venustiano Carranza, a provincial governor who had rebelled against Huerta in March 1914. Joined by other caudillos and their armies, Carranza's forces swept opposition aside as they moved south toward Mexico City. They entered the city in July and Huerta fled the country.

NOW THE REVOLUTION

For almost a century since obtaining independence, Mexicans had experienced political turmoil, several civil wars, and a lengthy dictatorship. Now they would become acquainted with a revolution, one still referred to in Mexico as The Revolution. Those who brought Huerta down eventually set out to construct a new power base and work extensive change in Mexico. The Constitution of 1917 outlined what those men had in mind.

The Constitution of 1917 provided for a president with a four-year term, later changed to six. A president could not succeed himself in office. The document also set up a congress and a judicial system. All land in Mexico, as well as the minerals beneath it, belonged to the people, that is, the government. The government could permit individual ownership if it wished. Education was compulsory for everyone between the ages of six and fifteen. And all schools were to be controlled by the government. The constitution granted workers the right to organize unions, bargain collectively, and strike. Workers were also promised an eight-hour day and a minimum wage. Child labor under age twelve was prohibited, and a Sunday holiday was provided.

Mexico's new constitution was a strong document. But whether it would be effective depended on the men who won government office.

Although he ruled Mexico as president until 1920, Carranza began and ended simply as a caudillo. He opposed many articles in the new constitution and he ran a corrupt, dictatorial regime. Ignoring the constitution, Carranza attempted to succeed himself in office. And in 1920 he was assassinated.

Álvaro Obregón, a rancher, became president of Mexico in 1920, followed in 1924 by Plutarco Calles, a former elementary school-teacher. Both men had fought against Huerta, and they proved more serious than Carranza about bringing change to Mexico. Obregón and Calles placed and maintained their own men in local, state, and national government positions. They built up a strong bureaucracy that depended on them for jobs. In addition, they kept the loyalty of the army by making sure generals were well fed, well paid, and well housed. They retired many army officers, replacing them with younger men who would develop with the Revolution.

Obregón and Calles built popular support in cities by organizing the trade union Confederación Regional Obrera Mexicana—Regional Confederation of Mexican Workers. This became known as CROM. It is true that CROM sometimes used rough tactics such as blackmail and intimidation of employers to achieve its goals. But the union did win higher wages and improved working conditions for millions of Mexicans. In the 1930s the Confederación de Trabajadores de México—the Confederation of Mexican Workers—replaced CROM. The CTM organized not only industrial laborers but white-collar workers as well.

To balance urban labor power, Revolution leaders created the Confederación Nacional de Campesinos—the National Peasant Confederation. Not only that. The government also set out to educate the masses. It spent a considerable amount of money to establish schools in rural areas, to train teachers, and to set up programs under which adults could learn to read and write. Today Mexico's literacy rate is around 85 percent. The government launched a drive also to improve health care in rural areas with hospitals, health education, and teams of nurses, doctors, and paramedics that circulated throughout the countryside.

The Revolution's land reform program began slowly. During the 1920s the government distributed only a few million acres, taken from the church and individual landholders, to peasant villages. The program picked up rapidly in the 1930s. It centered on *ejidos*, the tracts of village land that peasants held in common. On an ejido, each family was allowed to use a plot of fifteen to twenty acres, although many were smaller. Although families did not own the land, they could raise whatever crops they wished and use the produce themselves or sell it. The government also established ejido banks from which peasants could borrow money to buy seeds, fertilizer, farm tools, and equipment. In addition, the government launched irrigation projects. By the 1960s, ejidos contained about half of the land suitable for farming in Mexico.

Whether ejidos benefited Mexican peasants is a matter of dispute. The program did restore considerable land to mestizos and Indians whose villages once had owned it. Some observers believe that ejidos have been responsible for a better life for rural people. Critics have pointed out, however, that the small size of family plots has resulted in low crop yields per acre. Although half the rural population works on ejidos, they grow only 10 to 15 percent of the nation's crops. The rest is grown on small private farms and haciendas. Many ejidos are located on less productive land. And many peasants still use primitive agricultural methods. Only about 17 percent of Mexico's total land area can be used for growing crops. And with a steadily increasing population, that country faces a severe problem in producing enough food.

As part of the Revolution, the government encouraged the glorification of Mexico's Indian heritage, especially in painting and sculpture. José Clemente Orozco, Diego Rivera, David Alfaro Siqueiros, and other artists achieved fame during the 1920s and later with their huge murals and sculptures. It is true that at times they modified history to play down the Spanish contribution and to inspire Mexican nationalism. But they made great artistic contributions nonetheless.

THE COUNTERREVOLUTIONARIES

The Revolution was not without opposition. The Catholic church was especially critical of the government's land and educational policies. The criticism grew so pointed and severe that in 1926 President Calles deported about two hundred foreign priests and nuns. He closed the church schools and ordered native priests to register with civil authorities. Church officials struck back by calling a halt to all religious services in the nation on July 31, 1926. And armed rebellion led by a group of militant Catholics called Cristeros broke out in several states. Cristeros burned government schools and murdered teachers. Calles' government firmly put the Cristeros down. Alarmed by stories of Catholic persecution in Mexico, Catholics in the United States urged their government to intervene. President Calvin Coolidge refused, but he did send wealthy New York banker Dwight Whitney Morrow as ambassador to Mexico.

Eventually an agreement was pieced together, one part of which allowed religious instruction in all schools. In the summer of 1929 Mexican churches reopened.

The Revolution made foreign companies uneasy. They were especially worried about the article in the 1917 constitution placing land ownership in the hands of the people. Largely on that account, the United States refused to recognize the Obregón government for two years. After the United States seemed finally assured that the Mexican government planned no land takeovers, recognition was extended.

Foreign companies' status changed little until the 1930s. Then refinery and oil field workers struck for higher wages, an eight-hour day, paid vacations, and other benefits. Both sides took strong stands. Compromise became impossible. A Mexican supreme court decision called for a settlement mainly on the union's terms. The companies refused to budge. Insisting that foreigners, too, must obey Mexican laws, the government under President Lázaro Cárdenas in 1938 took over foreign oil company properties.

Cárdenas's action aroused a great hue and cry, particularly in the United States. Most Mexicans cheered the move; to them it represented the removal of a foreign yoke. After a period of confusion, Mexicans mastered oil technology, and when World War II broke out, Mexican oil was in great demand. In 1940 Mexico began paying foreign companies for the property the government had seized.

The church, hacendados, and foreign companies did not support the Revolution. But the army, labor, and the peasantry did. As a result, the country underwent extensive change. Mexican scholar Daniel Cosio Villegas emphasized this when he pointed out in 1961 that

> the landowner class, which held 60 to 70 percent of the country's entire wealth, disappeared; largely professional groups [executives, politicians, the army, university professors] were almost completely replaced; [there emerged] brand new collective owners of the land, the industrial worker, a popular army, and a new upper middle class so new, so tender, so fragile that not one of the thousand millionaires we have in Mexico has had his wealth over 20 to 30 years . . . not one of the great newspapers survived. Only two of about 50 banks continued under the new regime.

TODAY'S ONE-PARTY SYSTEM

Cárdenas was the last caudillo of the Revolution to become president. The real "caudillo" now was the revolutionary political party itself. Organized by Plutarco Calles in the late 1920s, the party today is known as PRI, Partido Revolucionario Institucional or Institutional Revolutionary party. With the PRI firmly in control, there no longer were pronunciamientos or revolts. The government changed every six years. Outgoing presidents often chose their successors.

Although a growing, but not united, opposition has been evident in recent elections, after more than sixty years, Mexico is still a one-party state. Most real contests for political office occur only within the PRI, not before the voters. There are usually opposition candidates for office, but they seldom, if ever, win. One-party rule does not mean that Mexicans do without political campaigns. Candidates appear before the voters to make speeches and attempt to learn voter attitudes and desires.

Not everyone, of course, is favorably impressed with the Mexican political system. Carlos Fuentes put these words in the mouth of one of his characters in his novel *Where the Air Is Clear:*

> I agree that our "one party" is better than the so-called opposition parties. But what I reject is the sleep our one party has imposed on Mexican politics . . . Which is the same as saying to the Mexican masses, You're quite well off as you are. Don't think, don't speak. We know what's best for you. Just be quiet. Isn't that precisely what Porfirio Díaz said?

Except for those who call for drastic changes in government and society, Mexicans enjoy freedom of speech and press. Freedom of religion exists in Mexico. At the very least, the Revolution united a country that had been divided into factions for a century. The church is not nearly as wealthy as it once was, and it suffers from a lack of priests and nuns to care for all its parishes and schools. But the church in Mexico is probably no worse off than in any country where church and state are separated. The Revolution produced a wider distribution of land than existed in 1910. And it made

Mexico the most industrialized nation in Latin America. The smog over Mexico City alone is ample testimony to that. Foreign investment, which the government sought actively from the 1940s on, has helped industrialization. And there has been considerable native investment as well. Mexican factories turn out steel products, chemicals, fertilizers, drugs, automobiles, and refrigerators. Mines produce silver, sulpher, lead, zinc, and coal as well as iron ore, and Mexico has become the world's fourth largest oil producer.

AN AGING REVOLUTION

Following the Cárdenas administration, which took over foreign oil companies and greatly encouraged unionization, the Revolution slowed down. In many ways it became conservative. Foreign investment was encouraged, and it increased. For example, United States investment in land, industry, and services climbed from $267 million in 1939 to over $1 billion in the 1960s. Latifundia did not entirely disappear in Mexico. Large landowners now were no longer hacendados, however. Many were middle-class businessmen who lived permanently in cities.

Although the Revolution aided the Mexican peasant, it was not by any means a peasant revolution. Peasants gained no political power. The Revolution was one of the bourgeoisie or middle class—professionals such as doctors and lawyers, merchants and shopkeepers, schoolteachers, and white-collar workers. They are the ones who benefited from the Revolution and, finally, from PRI stability.

During the 1950s and into the 1960s Mexicans enjoyed relative prosperity and quiet. The 1960s, however, proved to be a tumultuous decade over much of the world. There was a stirring of youth against the status quo and what was called the Establishment. Mexico, like a number of Latin American countries, had its share of demonstrations, particularly among intellectuals and students protesting the power of the PRI, police brutality, and an economy held tightly in the hands of the new elite. Events came to a climax in the Plaza de las Tres Culturas in Mexico City on October 2, 1968. Government troops fired on and killed a score of demonstrators. Many survivors were jailed.

In 1970, Luis Echeverría Alvarez became president. Under his administration, the government took a more open policy toward dissent. The Echeverría government released many political prisoners and encouraged political action in opposition to PRI.

José López Portillo was elected president of Mexico in 1976. Under his leadership, the government developed a ten-year plan aimed at increasing Mexico's industrial growth rate and reducing inflation and unemployment.

Oil would be the key to the plan, for by 1978 new discoveries had placed Mexico's proven oil and natural gas reserves at 37 billion barrels. This was almost triple previous estimates, and the actual amount might turn out to be even higher.

The term of President Miguel de la Madrid Hurtado, 1982 to 1988, was marked by economic problems. The world-wide recession of the early 1980s caused the demand for oil to decrease. Oil prices tumbled, as did Mexico's oil revenues. Without these expected revenues, Mexico had difficulty making payments on its large foreign debt. By the late 1980s, this debt was over $100 billion. In addition, over half of the work force was either unemployed or working only part time.

In the 1988 presidential election, Carlos Salinas de Gortari ran as the PRI candidate. Many Mexicans, weary of the PRI's failure to improve Mexico's economy, rallied around Cuauhtémoc Cárdenas, the son of Lazaro Cárdenas. After an election marred by charges of fraud, Salinas was declared the winner. However, he received only 51 percent of the vote, an unusually small amount for a PRI candidate. Cárdenas received 31 percent. The election suggests that Mexico's one-party system may be changing.

GIANTS OF LATIN AMERICAN LITERATURE

Chapter 7

Latin America has had its caudillos. It has also produced some of the great writers of our time. They have created prose and poetry of major importance, expressing the truths and doubts that have absorbed men and women throughout history and in all parts of the world.

Widely regarded as Latin America's finest contemporary poet is Chile's Pablo Neruda (1904–73). Winner of the Nobel Prize for literature in 1971, Neruda was actively involved in Marxist causes and served as the Chilean ambassador to France. His finest writing is not openly political, however, but instead expresses his deep feeling for his country and for the common people. As a child, Neruda lived in Temuco, then a frontier town in a region of lakes and rivers fed by the snows of the Andes. The brief story "A Pine Cone, A Toy Sheep . . ." is a sensitive recreation of Neruda's childhood world.

A PINE CONE, A TOY SHEEP . . .

I'll tell you a story about birds. On Lake Budi some years ago, they were hunting down the swans without mercy. The procedure was to approach them stealthily in little boats and then rapidly—very rapidly —row into their midst. Swans like albatrosses [large seabirds] have difficulty in flying; they must skim the surface of the water at a run. In the first phase of their flight they raise their big wings with great effort. It is then that they can be seized; a few blows with a bludgeon finish them off.

Someone made me a present of a swan: more dead than alive. It was of a marvelous species I have never seen anywhere else in the world: a black-throated swan—a snow boat with a neck packed, as it were, into a tight stocking of black silk. Orange-beaked, red-eyed.

This happened near the sea, in Puerto Saavedra, Imperial del Sur.

They brought it to me half-dead. I bathed its wounds and pressed little pellets of bread and fish into its throat; but nothing stayed down. Nevertheless the wounds slowly healed, and the swan came to regard me as a friend. At the same time, it was apparent to me that the bird was wasting away with nostalgia. So, cradling the heavy burden in my arms through the streets, I carried it down to the river. It paddled a few strokes, very close to me. I had hoped it might learn how to fish for itself, and pointed to some pebbles far below, where they flashed in the sand like the silvery fish of the South. The

Opposite: A mining village founded in colonial days as seen by Honduran painter Antonio José Velásquez. Detail from *View of San Antonio de Oriente, 1957.*

swan looked at them remotely, sad-eyed.

For the next twenty days or more, day after day, I carried the bird to the river and toiled back with it to my house. It was almost as large as I was. One afternoon it seemed more abstracted than usual, swimming very close and ignoring the lure of the insects with which I tried vainly to tempt it to fish again. It became very quiet; so I lifted it into my arms to carry it home again. It was breast high, when I suddenly felt a great ribbon unfurl, like a black arm encircling my face: it was the big coil of the neck, dropping down.

It was then that I learned swans do not sing at their death, if they die of grief.

I have said little about my poems. I know very little about such things, really. I prefer instead to move among the evocations [imaginative recreations] of my childhood. Perhaps, out of these plants and these solitudes and this violent life come the truths and the secret things—the profoundest *Poetics* of all, unknown because no one has written them down. We come upon poetry a step at a time, among the beings and things of this world: nothing is taken away without adding to the sum of all that exists in a blind extension of love.

Once, looking for little trophies and creaturely things of my world in the back of our house in Temuco, I came on a knothole in a neighboring fence post. I peered through the opening and saw a plot very like our own, all wilderness and waste. I withdrew a few steps, with the vague sense of portents to come. Suddenly a hand appeared—the tiny hand of a child just my age. I came closer, and the hand disappeared; in its place was a lovely white sheep—a toy sheep of nondescript wool. The wheels had fallen away— but that only made it more lifelike. I have never seen a more ravishing animal. I peered through the knothole, but the child was nowhere in sight. I went back to the house and returned with a prize of my own which I left in the very same spot: a pine cone I treasured above all things, half-open, balsamic, sweet-smelling. I left it there and I went away with the little toy sheep . . .

Left: Nineteenth century figurine from Peru.

Right: *Head of an Indian Woman.* Lithograph by Luis Arenal.

The following poem reveals the mature Neruda, regarding his country and the world:

LAZYBONES

They will continue wandering,
these things of steel among the stars,
and weary men will still go up
to brutalize the placid moon.
There, they will found their pharmacies.

In this time of the swollen grape,
the wine begins to come to life
between the sea and the mountain ranges.

In Chile now, cherries are dancing,
the dark mysterious girls are singing,
and in guitars, water is shining.

The sun is touching every door
and making wonder of the wheat.

The first wine is pink in color,
is sweet with the sweetness of a child,
the second wine is able-bodied,
strong like the voice of a sailor,
the third wine is a topaz, is
a poppy and a fire in one.

My house has both the sea and the earth,
my woman has great eyes
the color of wild hazelnut,
when night comes down, the sea
puts on a dress of white and green,
and later the moon in the spindrift foam
dreams like a sea-green girl.

I have no wish to change my planet.

Chile's earlier Nobel laureate was the poet Gabriela Mistral (1889–1957). A rural schoolteacher for twenty years, Mistral also traveled widely as an educator and as Chile's consul in Spain. She won the Nobel Prize in 1945. Frequently, as in the following poem, she expresses some of the inmost concerns of women:

FEAR

I do not want them to turn
my child into a swallow;
she might fly away into the sky
and never come down again to my doormat;
or nest in the eaves where my hands
could not comb her hair.
I do not want them to turn
my child into a swallow.

I do not want them to make
my child into a princess.
In tiny golden slippers how could
she play in the field?
And when night came, no longer
would she lie by my side.
I do not want them to make
my child into a princess.

And I would like even less
that one day they crown her queen.
They would raise her to a throne
where my feet could not climb.
I could not rock her to sleep
when nighttime came.
I do not want them to make
my child into a queen.

Alfonsina Storni of Argentina is another contemporary poet. Storni (1892–1938), a schoolteacher as well as a journalist, frequently tells what it is like to be a woman in a society dominated by men:

SHE WHO UNDERSTANDS

Her dark head fallen forward in her grief,
The beauteous woman kneels in suppliant
  fashion—
A woman past her youth; the dying Christ
From the stern rood [cross] looks on her
  with compassion.

A burden of vast sadness in her eyes,
Beneath her heart a child, a burden human.
Before the white Christ bleeding there she
  prays:
"Lord, do not let my child be born a
  woman!"

Jorge Luis Borges (1899–) of Argentina writes both prose and poetry on a wide range of subjects. Often describing a kind of journey toward self-discovery, Borges sees a world that is at once poetic, humorous, and tragic, a world where "any man is all men." In the following narrative, Borges tells of an event during the rule of Juan Manuel de Rosas, dictator of Argentina from 1835 to 1852. Rosas wanted Argentina to remain a loose federation of provinces. His henchmen, the *mazorca,* tried to rid Argentina of the Unitarians, who were in favor of national unity.

PEDRO SALVADORES

TO JUAN MURCHISON

I want to leave a written record (perhaps the first to be attempted) of one of the strangest and grimmest happenings in Argentine history. To meddle as little as possible in the telling, to abstain from picturesque details or personal conjectures is, it seems to me, the only way to do this.

A man, a woman, and the overpowering shadow of a dictator are the three characters. The man's name was Pedro Salvadores; my grandfather Acevedo saw him days or weeks after the dictator's downfall in the battle of Caseros. Pedro Salvadores may have been no different from anyone else, but the years and his fate set him apart. He was a gentleman like many other gentlemen of his day. He owned (let us suppose) a ranch in the country and, opposed to the tyranny, was on the Unitarian side. His wife's family name was Planes; they lived together on Suipacha Street near the corner of Temple in what is now the heart of Buenos Aires. The house in which the event took place was much like any other, with its street door, long arched entranceway, inner grillwork gate, its rooms, its row of two or three patios. The dictator, of course, was Rosas.

One night, around 1842, Salvadores and his wife heard the growing, muffled sound of horses' hooves out on the unpaved street and the riders shouting their drunken *vivas* and their threats. This time Rosas' henchmen did not ride on. After the shouts came repeated knocks at the door; while the men began forcing it, Salvadores was able to pull the dining-room table aside, lift the rug, and hide himself down in the cellar. His wife dragged the table back in place. The *mazorca* broke into the house; they had come to take Salvadores. The woman said her husband had run away to Montevideo. The men did not believe her; they flogged her, they smashed all the blue chinaware (blue was the Unitarian color), they searched the whole house, but they never thought of lifting the rug. At midnight they rode away, swearing that they would soon be back.

Here is the true beginning of Pedro Salvadores' story. He lived nine years in the cellar. For all we may tell ourselves that years are made of days and days of hours and that nine years is an abstract term and an impossible sum, the story is nonetheless gruesome. I suppose that in the darkness, which his eyes somehow learned to decipher, he had no particular thoughts, not even of his hatred or his danger. He was simply there—in the cellar—with echoes of the world he was cut off from sometimes reaching him from overhead: his wife's footsteps, the bucket clanging against the lip of the well, a heavy rainfall in the patio. Every day of his imprisonment, for all he knew, could have been the last.

His wife let go all the servants, who could possibly have informed against them, and told her family that Salvadores was in Uruguay. Meanwhile, she earned a living for them both sewing uniforms for the army. In the course of time, she gave birth to two children; her family turned from her, thinking she had a lover. After the tyrant's fall, they got down on their knees and begged to be forgiven.

What was Pedro Salvadores? Who was he? Was it his fear, his love, the unseen presence of Buenos Aires, or—in the long run—habit that held him prisoner? In order to keep him with her, his wife would make up news to tell him about whispered plots and rumored victories. Maybe he was a coward and she loyally hid it from him that she knew. I picture him in his cellar perhaps without a candle, without a book. Darkness probably sank him into sleep. His dreams, at the outset, were probably of that sudden night when the blade sought his throat, of the streets he knew so well, of the open plains. As the years went on, he would have been unable to escape even in his sleep; whatever he dreamed would have taken place in the cellar. At first, he may have been a man hunted down, a man in danger of his life; later (we will never know for certain), an animal at peace in its burrow or a sort of dim god.

All this went on until that summer day of 1852 when Rosas fled the country. It was only then that the secret man came out into the light of day; my grandfather spoke with him. Flabby, overweight, Salvadores was the color of wax and could not speak above a low voice. He never got back his confiscated lands; I think he died in poverty.

As with so many things, the fate of Pedro Salvadores strikes us as a symbol of something we are about to understand, but never quite do.

In the following poem, Borges describes the world of the Argentinean cowhands known as gauchos. The names in the sixth last stanza are those of gaucho chiefs. Justo José de Urquiza had been the principal field commander under Rosas but turned against him.

THE GAUCHOS

Who was there to tell them their forebears came from across the seas? Who was there to tell them what a sea and its waters are like?

Offspring of the white man, they looked down on him; offspring of the red man, they were his enemies.

Many of them, if they ever heard the word *gaucho,* heard it only as an insult.

They learned the paths of the stars, the habits of the air and birds, and what clouds from the south and a red ring around the moon foretell.

They were herders of wild cattle and sure riders of the desert horse they had broken that morning. They were rope throwers, branders, foremen, drovers, the men who made up the posse, and from time to time the outlaw who fought them. One—the man listened to—was the ballad singer.

He never hurried his song, for dawn is long in coming, and he never raised his voice.

Some were farmhands who doubled as jaguar hunters; a poncho wound around the left arm for a shield, the right hand sank the knife into the animal's belly as it sprang on its hind legs.

Leisurely talk, maté [a bitter herb tea], and cards were the shape of their time.

Unlike so many peasants, irony came easily to them.

They were enduring, they were celibate [unmarried], they were poor. Hospitality was their happiness.

Now and then, Saturday night binges dragged them down.

They died and they killed with innocence.

They were not religious, apart from holding some dim superstition or other, but hardship taught them the cult of courage.

Men bred in cities made up a speech for them and a literature of rural metaphors.

Certainly they were not adventurers, though cattle drives might carry them long distances and wars farther still.

They did not give history a single caudillo.

They fought for López, for Ramírez, for Artigas, for Quiroga, for Bustos, for Pedro Campbell, for Rosas, for Urquiza, for Ricardo López Jordán (who had Urquiza knifed and shot down), for Peñaloza, and for Saravia.

They did not give their lives for their country—that abstraction—but for this or that landowner, or out of a fit of anger, or to the lure of danger.

Their mortal dust is scattered over the length and breadth of the continent—in republics whose history they knew nothing of, on battlefields now famous.

The poet Ascasubi saw them singing and fighting.

They lived out their lives as in a dream, without knowing who they were or what they were.

Maybe the case is the same for us all.

Painted Mexican pottery figures of a bride and groom.

Latin America has also produced some of the world's most widely read and admired novelists, particularly in the twentieth century: Carlos Fuentes of Mexico, Romulo Gallegos of Venezuela, and Gabriel García Márquez of Colombia. Foremost among them is Miguel Angel Asturias of Guatemala (1899–1974), who won the Nobel Prize in 1967. A poet as well as a novelist, Asturias studied Indian cultures and became a sympathetic interpreter of Indian life, as the following poem reveals. Mixco is a large Indian village near Guatemala City.

THE INDIANS COME DOWN FROM MIXCO

The Indians come down from Mixco
laden with deep blue
and the city with its frightened
streets receives them
with a handful of lights
that, like stars, are extinguished
when daybreak comes.

A sound of heartbeats
is in their hands that stroke
the wind like two oars;
and from their feet fall
prints like little soles
in the dust of the road.

The stars that peep out
at Mixco stay in Mixco
because the Indians catch them
for baskets that they fill
with chickens and the big white flowers
of the golden Spanish bayonet.

The life of the Indians
is quieter than ours,
and when they come down from Mixco
they make no sound but the panting
that sometimes hisses on their lips
like a silken serpent.

Many critics consider Uruguayan Horacio Quiroga (1878–1937) the best short-story writer of South America. Quiroga spent many years in the rain forest along the Upper Paraná River. He was a keen observer of the struggle there between man and nature and a great teller of animal tales, such as this one:

THE FLAMINGOS' STOCKINGS

Once upon a time the vipers [poisonous snakes] gave a big dance. They invited the frogs and the toads, the flamingos, and the alligators and the fish. Each alligator, in order to dress up, had put a banana necklace around its neck and came smoking Paraguayan cigars.

The frogs had perfumed their whole bodies, and they arrived on two feet. Besides that, each one wore a firefly hanging like a lamp and swinging back and forth. And the most splendid of all were the coral snakes, who arrived wearing long filmy dresses of red, white, and black, and when they danced they looked like variegated [streaked with different colors] streamers.

Only the flamingos, who at that time had white legs, were sad. They had so little intelligence that they didn't know how to make themselves look pretty. They envied the dresses of all the rest and especially those of the coral snakes. Each time a snake passed in front of them coquetting and swirling her sheer skirt, the flamingos nearly died of envy. Then one flamingo said:

"I know what we should do. Let's put on red, black, and white stockings, and the coral snakes will fall in love with us."

Flying off together, they crossed the river and went knocking at the door of a store in town.

"Knock-knock!" sounded their feet on the wood.

"Who is it?" asked the storekeeper.

"We are the flamingos. Do you have any red, black, and white colored stockings?"

The storekeeper answered:

"What are you talking about? Red, black, and white? There aren't any stockings like that anywhere. Who are you?"

"We're flamingos," they replied.

And the man said:

"Then for sure you're crazy flamingos." And the man chased them away with a broom.

The flamingos went to all of the stores, and everywhere people thought they were crazy.

Then an armadillo that had gone to the river for a drink of water, wanted to play a joke on the flamingos, so he said, with a sweeping bow:

"Good evening, distinguished flamingos! I know what you're looking for. You won't find stockings like that in any store around here. Maybe there are some in Buenos Aires, but you would have to have them shipped here by parcel post. My sister-in-law, the barn owl, has stockings like that. Ask her, and she'll provide you with red, black, and white stockings, I'm sure."

The flamingos thanked him, and they flew away to the cave of the barn owl. There they told her:

"Good evening, barn owl! We've come to ask you for some red, black, and white stockings. Today is the big snake ball, and if we wear pretty stockings like those, the coral snakes will fall in love with us."

"I'll be glad to help you!" said the barn owl. "Wait a second and I'll be back right away."

She flew away and left the flamingos alone. And soon she returned with the stockings. Only they were not stockings. They were beautiful skins from coral snakes that the barn owl had recently caught.

"Here are your stockings," the barn owl told them. "You have only one thing to worry about: Be sure to dance all night, and don't stop for a minute, for if you do, you'll be crying instead of dancing."

But the flamingos, being so stupid, didn't realize their great danger, and crazy with happiness they put their legs through the tubes of the coral snake skins, like stockings. And they went flying off happily to the dance.

When those at the dance saw the flamingos arrive wearing their beautiful stockings, they were full of envy. All the snakes wanted to dance just with them, and since the flamingos kept their legs in motion all the time, the snakes couldn't very well see what those beautiful stockings were made of.

The coral snakes especially were very upset. They did not take their eyes off the stockings. They squatted almost to the floor in their efforts to get a good look, and tried to touch the legs of the flamingos with their tongues, because a snake's tongue is like the hand of a person. But the flamingos danced and danced, and never stopped even though they were so tired that they could hardly move.

Realizing this, the coral snakes immediately begged the frogs for flashlights, the fireflies they wore around their necks. And they all waited together until the flamingos should drop from exhaustion. As a matter of fact, a moment later, a flamingo that couldn't dance any longer staggered and fell down. Instantly the coral snakes rushed up with their lamps, and got a good look at the legs of the flamingos. They saw what the stockings really were, and they hissed so loudly that it was heard all the way across the Paraná River.

"They aren't stockings," screamed the snakes. "We know what they are! The flamingos have killed our sisters, and are wearing their skins for stockings."

On hearing that, the flamingos, frightened at being discovered, tried to fly away, but they were so tired they couldn't even lift one leg. So the coral snakes attacked them. Wrapping themselves around the legs of the flamingos, they tried to chew off the stockings. Furiously they tore them off in pieces, at the same time biting the legs of the birds and trying to kill them.

The flamingos, crazy with pain, jumped back and forth trying to shake off the coiled coral snakes. Finally, seeing that there wasn't a single piece of stocking left, the snakes let the flamingos go, being exhausted themselves. They went away smoothing out the sheer fabric of their dresses. Besides, the coral snakes were sure that the flamingos would die, because half, at least, of the coral snakes that had bitten them were of the poisonous variety.

But the flamingos did not die. They dashed into the water, as a relief for their extreme pain. They screamed with agony. Their legs, that had been white, were now crimsoned by the venom of the snakes. They spent day after day standing in the water, continually suffering from the terrible pain in their legs, which were now blood red because of the snake poison.

That was a long time ago, and yet even today the flamingos spend most of the day with their red legs immersed in water, trying to ease the burning pain. Occasionally they leave the water's edge, and walk a few steps onto the ground in order to see how they feel. But the pain of the poison soon returns and they hurry back into the water. At times the agony that they feel is so great that they raise one leg and stay that way for hours, because they can't extend it.

This is the story of the flamingos, who used to have white legs, but now they are red.

Some writers of prose and poetry have glorified their nations, looking forward with great optimism to the future. One of these was the Brazilian Ronald de Carvalho, who speaks of his country in the following poem. In the second stanza, Ouro-Preto, Baía, Congonhas, and Sabará are cities of Brazil.

BRAZIL

. . .

I hear the vast song of Brazil!

. . .

I hear all Brazil singing, humming, calling, shouting!
Hammocks swaying,
whistles blowing,
factories grinding, pounding, panting, screaming, howling and snoring,
cylinders exploding,
cranes revolving,
wheels turning,
rails trembling,
noises of foothills and plateaus, cattlebells, neighings, cowboy songs, and lowings,
chiming of bells, bursting of rockets,
Ouro-Preto, Baía, Congonhas, Sabará,
clamour of stock-exchanges shrieking numbers like parrots,
tumult of streets that seethe beneath skyscrapers,
voices of all the races that the wind of the seaports tosses into the jungle!

. . .

But what I hear, above all, in this hour of pure sunlight

. . .

is the song of thy cradles, Brazil, of all thy cradles, in which there sleeps, mouth dripping with milk, dusky, trusting, the man of tomorrow!

LATIN LIFE-STYLES

In Latin America one finds differences among people from country to country and from class to class. Still, one can ignore national and class boundaries and speak of a Latin American culture. It consists of attitudes and world views that set Latin Americans off from other peoples.

Latin American society is male-dominated. It is also a Catholic society. Whether they attend mass regularly or not, most Latin Americans consider themselves faithful Catholics.

Family ties are strong. Regardless of what other roles a Latin American might play, that of family member is all-important. And, where the family consists of father, mother, and children, the father is the head. He is obeyed and deferred to. The feeling of family carries over into business and government. Family members and relatives receive first consideration with respect to jobs and favors.

Latin Americans have traditionally been individualists, sometimes fiercely so. They are not much for teamwork as a rule. Government and politics are personal matters and matters of personality. Government in Latin America, as elsewhere, has spawned bureaucracy. But Latin Americans often deal with a bureaucracy in personal terms. They seek within it some individual with whom they can deal. When it comes to political leaders, the Latin American prefers the energetic, self-confident, and dramatic person. Party politics is a matter of personalities rather than one of programs and ideologies. Loyalty is to an individual.

Generally speaking, Latin Americans are not backslappers. They do not care for casual intimacy and first-name relationships except among close friends. They value *dignidad*—dignity. Practical jokes often go against the grain.

In most parts of Latin America, the business day begins late. It also ends late. The daily after-lunch *siesta* or rest period is common. Dinner has traditionally been served at nine or later in the evening. This indicates a leisurely life-style, not necessarily a lack of interest in material things. Generally speaking, however, Latin

Opposite: An aristocratic Peruvian family, Juan de Aliaga, his wife and children, seated in the dining room of their home in Lima.

Americans view money and other possessions as things to enjoy, not things to hoard or be stingy with.

The culture rests on a traditional aristocratic base. The pace is set by the wealthy, who value graciousness, accommodation, and leisure, and who abhor working with their hands. In practice, the society rests on a broad base of the poor, who perform necessary labor, and on a middle class. But it is the cultural traits of the upper class that in large part flavor the entire society.

Generalizations about Latin American culture are valid. Yet they do, of course, disguise important details. They tell little specifically about the region's rich variety of people. Certain similarities bind them together; certain differences set them apart. This becomes apparent as one examines a Mayan group, ranchers of northern Brazil, the people of a small town in Colombia, and various urban groups.

Opposite: A Mexican woman making tortillas, for centuries the staple food of the lower classes.

DESCENDANTS OF THE MAYA

In the state of Chiapas, Mexico, live some eight thousand Maya, descendants of the civilization that flourished in pre-Columbian times. They reside in a governmental unit called the *municipio* of Zinacantan. About four hundred Indians live in the central town of Zinacantan. The rest live in fifteen surrounding hamlets. The Zinacantecos come to town to trade, to observe religious ceremonies and festivals, and to take part in local government affairs. Their pattern of life is a blend of Mayan and Spanish.

DAILY LIFE

For the women of a Zinacanteco household, the day begins before dawn. They are up to start the fire and make breakfast.

First the women boil maize in lime water. Once the kernels are soft, they grind them into meal. Then they pat the meal into round, flat tortilla shapes and fry them on a concave clay or metal plate, about thirty seconds to a side. The tortillas are kept warm in a clay jar. Usually about two hours are needed to prepare enough meal for the tortillas that will be consumed that day. In the meantime, a pot of beans is cooking.

Shortly after dawn, men and boys are up. By eight o'clock enough tortillas are ready for breakfast. Seated on tiny chairs around the fire in the one-room hut, the men and boys dip tortillas into the bean pot to scoop up a filling, then wash their food down with cups of hot, sweetened coffee. When the men and boys have had their fill, the women and girls breakfast on what remains.

Following the morning meal, males and females go about their separate tasks. What the men and older boys do depends on the season and on whether they labor in the highlands or the lowlands. Most of the work consists of planting, tending, and harvesting crops.

Maize is the principal crop. Fields are cleared of brush and rubble in the late winter dry season. In the highlands, Zinacanteco farmers use digging sticks to prepare the soil for planting in March. In the lowlands, planting is delayed until summer rains begin in May. In both areas, fields are hoed free from weeds twice, during the summer months of June and July. Weeding is hard work. It begins soon after dawn each day and lasts until four or so in the afternoon. In the lowlands, harvest time is October; in the highlands, November and into December. Once harvested, the corn is dried, shelled, and stored.

Zinacantecos also grow beans and squash.

Opposite: Zinacantecos dressed in traditional finery: white serapes with red stripes, leather shoulder pouches, and beribboned sombreros. The men oil their legs when coming to town.

Almost every family has a flock of a dozen or so chickens which are kept for their eggs. Chicken is usually eaten only on ceremonial occasions.

When not busy with growing crops, Zinacanteco men mend fences, repair and sharpen tools, or take produce to the central town market for sale.

The women and older girls care for the younger children. They gather firewood. They weave woolen and sometimes cotton threads into cloth and make clothing. They prepare meals. Nearly every household has a flock of sheep. At night the sheep remain in small corrals. Each morning, the girls take them out to graze. The girls carry with them small portable looms on which to weave as they watch over the animals. Zinacantecos keep sheep for their wool, not for meat.

Tortillas and beans form the midday meal. Like breakfast, it is eaten in the hut, unless the men are working too far away. Then tortillas and beans are carried to them. The third meal of the day, containing much the same food as the others, comes at sundown. Usually by eight in the evening, everyone is asleep.

BIRTH AND GROWING UP

Each stage of Zinacanteco life—birth, marriage, and death—is attended by ceremony. A midwife presides over birth. And within an hour after it is born, the baby is presented with objects that symbolize its sex. Boys are shown a digging stick, an axe, and a hoe. Girls are presented with implements for grinding corn and with parts of a back-strap, portable loom. On the second day, all members of the household receive the baby, embrace and kiss it, and blow in both of its ears.

Usually within a month, certainly within three or four months, the baby is baptized. The ceremony mixes Catholic and Zinacanteco ritual.

The baptismal rite may be performed either in the Church of San Lorenzo in Zinacantan or at the Cathedral in San Cristóbal where a priest is always on duty. On the appointed day, the father picks up the godparents and the two couples go to the Church with the infant. Two white candles are purchased, one to be held by each godparent. At the Church the candles are lighted, the infant is transferred to the godparent of the same sex, while each godparent holds a candle. The priest then recites a prayer, places a piece of salt in the infant's mouth, makes the sign of the cross over the forehead, mouth, and chest, and touches the infant's head with his stole and bathes it in Holy Water. The infant has now been through all the necessary Catholic ritual, but the Zinacanteco ritual continues. The godparents return home with the parents and are served a formal ritual meal which is normally attended by the grandparents and other close relatives, and sometimes friendly neighbors as well. In the Zinacanteco view, these persons all become ritual kinsmen of the new godparents.

The moment that the new social link is established, the persons who address each other as *kumpare* and *kumale* (in Tzotzil [the Zinacanteco language]) acquire special lifetime rights and obligations toward one another. For a man, a *compadre* [godfather] can be called upon to loan money, help build a house, become an assistant in a ceremony, or assist in political crises. For a woman, a *comadre* [godmother] may be called upon to loan money, help make tortillas on ritual occasions, or serve as a confidante in an exchange of gossip. For both men and women, the relationship is important for hospitality that is offered when one is traveling. In a word, the *compadrazgo* network [between a child's parents and godparents] provides a pool of people to whom one can turn for money, labor, credit, political support, and hospitality.

New members of a Zinacanteco household are treated gently and with much affection. Toilet training is not severe, and a child is frequently not weaned until it is replaced at the mother's breast by a new baby. Sometimes this may not occur until a child is three years old.

Girls begin training for household tasks at an early age. By age seven or eight, they make substantial contributions to running the household. Boys, on the other hand, are cut off from male tasks until about age nine. They might perform a few "female" tasks around the house, such as gathering firewood. Or they might run errands or simply play with their fellows. Actually, they are more or less just in the way. At age nine, however, they begin to help in the fields. By age twelve or fourteen, boys play an important part in growing food.

Few Zinacanteco children attend school, although schooling is available. Most parents consider it unimportant. For boys, learning at least a little Spanish is valuable, for they will need it later when dealing with *Ladinos*—mestizos—in the market place. But they do not need a great deal. Besides Spanish, children who attend school for three years or so learn to read and write and do arithmetic, and they learn Mexican history.

COURTSHIP AND MARRIAGE

Courtship and marriage mark the next stage of life. For both boys and girls, courtship begins in the early or middle teens. And it is accompanied by a rather complicated ritual.

When a Zinacanteco boy reaches the age of sixteen to seventeen, he begins to think of marriage and to look over the available girls from among those that he sees along the paths, at fiestas, or visiting in the homes of relatives. . . .

The first step in courtship is for the boy to persuade his parents that he has made a wise choice and enlist their aid in the expenses that will follow. The boy and the parents then select two "petitioners," respected men who have the reputation for being good speakers, and enlist their services by calling upon them with bottles of liquor. Meanwhile, the boy busies himself learning all that he can about the daily habits and future plans of his chosen girl's father, as he will use this information to plan the strategy for the formal petition.

On the appointed day of the petition, the two petitioners and their wives come to the boy's house when they are told, for the first time, the name of the girl who has been selected. Secrecy is necessary so that the father of the girl will not hear of the impending petition and leave home to avoid giving away his daughter.

The boy's family, accompanied by the petitioners, walks to the girl's house. The boy's mother carries a basket of gifts, including chocolate, brown sugar, and rolls, and the boy carries a 20-liter jug of rum. Arriving at the girl's house well after dark, they wait quietly outside while assistants surround the house. One of the petitioners then calls to the people inside, asking to borrow a pine torch or an axe, or making some other request that will get the door open. Then the petitioners and their wives rush inside, while the girl's family attempts to escape through the back door, only to be stopped by the helpers. The petitioners then kneel in front of the girl's father, place bottles of liquor at his feet, and begin their request, while the women in the boy's group plead with the girl's mother. Since the phrases are traditional, both sides talk at once, without listening carefully to each

Zapotec woman grinding corn on a stone *metate,* unchanged since the days of her early ancestors.

The pleading continues through the long night, as the drink-pourer tries to serve liquor to the father of the girl, and the petitioners take turns on their knees on the hard earthen floor. The father of the girl steadfastly refuses the liquor.

Finally, the father gives in and accepts his first shot of liquor, and the long courtship formally begins. The petitioners move from their kneeling position to chairs, and the boy is brought in to meet his future father-in-law. The boy kneels, asks pardon for having come into the house, and promises in a long speech to be a good son-in-law. He then serves the girl's father and all her relatives a shot of liquor, and the drinking continues until the jug is empty. . . . From this point on, the boy begins to use kin terms to address his future wife's family, but he is the only one to enter into the web of kinship at this time. The early phases of courtship are a trial period, and if it doesn't work out, the only kin tie that must be severed [cut] is that between the boy and his fiancée's family.

other. The only person who is silent is the girl, who sits apart with her eyes downcast and her shawl drawn over her mouth.

A typical dialogue follows:

The petitioners: "May your head speak, may your heart speak. Seize my words, beloved father (or mother). Today I speak because of your mud, your earth (metaphorical way of referring to the girl). Don't cut out my child's heart." The father (or mother) of girl: "Your child is a devil, he drinks too much. I won't give my child. I won't give her to suffering, to beating, to scolding. With difficulty I raised her, talked to her. Get out! Leave! If I want, I'll look for you with words. Get out! Leave! Take your water (liquor)!"

Courtship is expensive for a young man. Over the following months he gradually pays a brideprice in the form of fruit and rum, maize and tortillas, and work in his future father-in-law's fields. The boy's father helps pay the brideprice, which puts the boy in debt to him.

When the father of the bride-to-be decides that her suitor has invested enough in her—which may not be until two years have passed—the time has come for the "house entering" ceremony. Here members of both families gather in the girl's family house to share food and complete the courtship process.

Bride and groom go through three wedding ceremonies. One is civil, performed by a local government official. The next is religious, held in the Catholic church. The final ceremony is traditional, taking place in the groom's family house. Here ritual centers on receiving the bride into her new home.

The whole process of courtship and marriage involves an exchange of individuals, goods, services, entertainment, and courtesies. It serves to bind two families together.

Many Zinacantecos cannot afford all the elements of traditional courtship and marriage. They must trim corners. They might shorten the courtship period, reduce the brideprice, or cut down on elaborate ceremonies. Some couples simply elope. But even so, the groom or his family must pay the bride's family some kind of brideprice.

Because of brideprice, a newly married man is indebted to his father. Consequently he works for a number of years not only to support his wife but also to repay the cost of courtship and marriage. A young Zinacanteco couple ordinarily do not look forward to moving from the man's family home into one of their own until they are in their mid-twenties. The new wife spends several years under her mother-in-law's domination.

THE CARGO SYSTEM

Participation in what is known as the *cargo* system is an important part of a Zinacanteco male's life. "Cargo" refers to positions in religious ceremonies which are a mixture of ancient Mayan religion and Catholicism. To a large extent, the system revolves around caring for the images of saints and performing rituals involving the saints. This takes place in a Ceremonial Center, a gardenlike arrangement near the Catholic church in Zinacantan. Cargo positions carry a great deal of prestige.

There are four cargo levels. Ideally a man serves a year at each one. The lowest level is that occupied by *mayores* and *mayordomos.* Twelve mayores serve as policemen and as errand runners for local government officials. They also perform minor ceremonial func-

tions. Twenty-eight mayordomos care for the images of certain saints, decorating them with flowers, for example.

At the next cargo level are fourteen *alféreces.* These men are also responsible for taking care of saints' images, but they spend much of their year in office taking part in ritual meals and dancing for the saints.

Next come *regidores,* of which there are four. Among their duties is that of collecting money to pay priests for saying masses. At the very top of the cargo system are *alcaldes viejos,* or old alcaldes, of which there are three. One is a very old man whose position is honorary. The regidores and alcaldes together are known as the Elders. They manage the entire cargo system.

To enter the system, a man presents his application and a bottle of rum to the Elders. His name is then placed on a waiting list. Once each year he must reaffirm his intention. If he does not, his name is removed from the list. A number of years may pass while a man awaits his turn to serve, but being on the cargo list carries a great deal of prestige in itself.

Cargo positions can be expensive. They require a man to furnish food, rum, candles, fireworks, incense, and other ceremonial items. A year's service as a mayordomo may cost a man as much as fourteen thousand pesos, or about $1,200. To pay the cost of serving, a man must manage his fields well, producing crops to sell. He must, in addition, possess sufficient relatives from whom he can borrow money. Not infrequently, once a man completes one cargo position, he must work for a time to repay debts and accumulate more money before he can move on to the next position.

Cargoholders are responsible for rituals and ceremonies performed at the Ceremonial Center. They also participate in fiestas that are geared to the Catholic calendar of saints' days, including such festivals as Christmas and Easter. There are thirty-five fiestas from December 31 to the following Christmas. Seven of them honor saints special to the Zinacantecos, such as San Lorenzo. Fiestas frequently last three or more days.

Christmas, like Easter, is a very special fiesta. The Christmas season begins on December 15 and continues until January 6.

The ritual sequence begins with a flower renewal by the Mayordomos in their houses and in the churches. There follows a period of nine days (December 16 to 24) when the Mayordomos gather in front of the church of San Lorenzo each morning to eat sweetened squash to commemorate the nine months of the Virgin's pregnancy. During the same period the Mayordomos and Sacristáns perform the posada (inn) ceremony to commemorate the narrative of Joseph and Mary seeking lodging at many inns before the birth of the Christ child.

On December 23 the Mayordomos and their assistants construct an enormous, beautiful crèche [Nativity scene] in the church of San Lorenzo. The corners of the crèche are large, freshly cut pine trees, and the walls and roof are made of pine boughs. The edges of the walls and roof are decorated with streamers of red, white, and orange flowers, and the crib is placed inside.

On December 24 a reed mat "bull" is constructed which will become the focus of dancing and fun-making in the dance drama. The "bull" is carried over the head and shoulders of a man, and it performs with two married couples (the males are masked and ride stick horses, while their spouses are unmasked) impersonated by the Mayordomos taking turns. The performance is watched by two young boys dressed as "angels." During the next twelve days the drama is repeated over and over; the "bull" attacks the husbands, while their wives [try] to "tame" the "bull." Finally, the "bull" gores and kills the husbands who are revived when their wives take them to a high official who rubs their bodies . . . with the rattles they have been using in the dance.

At midnight on Christmas Eve, the birth of the Christ children (there are two in Zinacantan belief: one older brother and one younger brother) is reenacted in the church of San Sebastian. The two children are carried by their godparents—the Alcaldes, the Regidores, and the top civil officials from the Cabildo [town hall]—to the church of San Lorenzo where they are placed in the crèche. All come forward to venerate [show devotion to] them to the resonant sound of turtle shell drums.

The ritual sequence ends on January 6th with the chasing, capture, and killing of the "bull." The boy "angels" who have passively watched the drama up to this point, now lasso the "bull" and he is killed by wooden knives plunged into his body. His "blood" (consisting of rum liquor with onions and chile to make it red) is passed around and drunk.

RITES OF THE DEAD

Ceremony surrounds Zinacantecos in death as well as in life. To Zinacantecos, natural death results from "soul loss."

One's animal spirit is let out of its corral, they believe. An older person washes the corpse and dresses it in clean clothes. Candles are lit. And as musicians play violins, guitars, and harps, the family holds an all-night wake. At dawn, family members eat a ritual meal.

On the way to the cemetery that day, the procession of mourners and wailers stops periodically. The coffin is opened. Candles are lit and prayers said. An old woman gives the corpse a drink, sprinkling water on its lips from a geranium. At the cemetery a grave is dug. While this goes on there are more prayers and the corpse is given additional drinks of water.

Once the grave is ready, the coffin is lowered half way. Then everyone participates in a round of rum. Finally, the coffin is lowered all the way. Each person steps forward to throw three handfuls of earth on top of it. The grave is filled and pine needles scattered on it. A small cross is erected at the head and two candles are lit.

Family members visit the grave for nine days following burial. Prayers are recited and more candles lit. The grave is frequently decorated, especially on All Souls' Day, November 2.

SETTLING DISPUTES

Religion is an intimate, almost everyday thing among the Zinacantecos. And they are close to their government too— not the national one in far distant Mexico City or the state government of Chiapas— but that concerned with the municipio.

Zinacantecos fill all but one local government office. The exception is that of secretary, which is filled by a Ladino. He does little save keep records. A village president (the *Presidente*), a *sindico* (collector of court fines), and four judges are elected to three-year terms.

Local officials greet and entertain higher visiting government officials. They collect money for such public projects as road and bridge building and repair. They supervise work on projects. Officials also perform a number of ritual functions, especially those connected with fiestas. But much of their time is spent settling disputes among hamlet residents.

While some Zinacantecos seek the Presidente out in his house at night so that they can have an uninterrupted hearing of their cases, the more common procedure is for the plaintiff to approach the Presidente at the Cabildo. The plaintiff bows to the Presidente and other officials in rank order, presents a bottle of rum, and describes his complaint. The Presidente and other officials listen, and, if persuaded, summon two of the Mayores [policemen] to go after the accused and bring him into the Cabildo. The defendant appears, also with a bottle of rum, bows to the officials, and presents his defense. Usually, both parties are accompanied by relatives known to be "good talkers" who serve as "lawyers." All of them talk at once, and one wonders how [with this uproar] a judgment is ever reached. Witnesses may be called on both sides to provide additional testimony.

The case may have one of three outcomes:

First, it may be settled in this Zinacanteco court. The officials help to the extent of expressing their approval of an argument or hooting with laughter at a defendant who is telling an obvious lie. In this case the culprit will be required to return the stolen property and be fined, or jailed, or both.

Second, the case may prove to be too serious for the Zinacanteco court to handle (for example, a case of murder). Then it will be passed along to Ladino officials in San Cristóbal.

Or third, it may be impossible to reach a clear-cut decision, even after all the testimony is heard. Then the Presidente's efforts are devoted to calming down the two parties so they will not bear grudges against each other and will be able to live harmoniously in the same hamlet.

The Zinacantecos use metal farming tools. They participate in a money economy, buying and selling in the market centers. Their religious ceremonies contain elements of Catholicism. But basically, Zinacanteco life has changed little over the centuries. It remains much as it was when Spaniards found it in the sixteenth century.

IN THE GRASSLANDS OF NORTHERN BRAZIL

Chapter 9

Parents of an infant born in the territory of Roraima in northern Brazil wish the child to be baptized as soon as possible.

The high infant mortality rate accounts for this. Few families fail to lose at least one child. And, according to traditional Catholic belief, the soul of an unbaptized infant resides in limbo, never reaching heaven. Since Roraima is a relatively isolated area, a visiting priest may not arrive until several months after a child has been born to administer this sacrament.

Life in Roraima depends on cattle. And caring for livestock is a male responsibility. Six-year-old boys take care of sheep, goats, and horses. By age ten, boys are expected to feed and milk cows. At age twelve, a boy is allowed to eat in the main room with the men instead of in the kitchen with the women. Finally, about two years later, a youth hangs his sleeping hammock in the bunkhouse. This marks his passage from childhood to maturity. Already he can ride well. And he now participates in daily ranch work with men and rides with them on cattle roundups and drives.

In Roraima girls do not work with cattle. They learn household tasks.

Schools in the rural areas of Roraima do not go beyond the elementary grades. Many children receive no schooling at all, largely be-cause their parents see little relationship between schooling and learning to ride a horse and care for a ranch. Should Roraima become less isolated and should scientific methods of ranching be introduced, this attitude might change.

Most young men in Roraima stay at home, working for their fathers until marriage. At that point the young man and his wife establish their own home, although the man may remain part of his father's ranch operation.

WINNING A BRIDE

Distance between the ranches makes the courtship period long and somewhat difficult. Girl-boy relationships are frequently formed, however, during roundup time. They also begin at dances that people from a wide area attend.

Most couples marry in their early twenties. Many marriages are common-law arrangements—that is, without benefit of either civil or religious ceremony. This is especially true among poorer people. In numerous instances, however, a common-law marriage is consecrated with a religious ceremony when a visiting priest arrives in the area. Some couples who marry formally go through a civil cere-

Opposite: His leather clothing protects the vaqueiro of northeastern Brazil against thornbush and scrub.

mony only. Among the average Roraimaenses, there is no elaborate ritual or celebration connected with marriage. Well-to-do ranchers, however, usually sponsor a party in Bôa Vista, the territory's capital on the Branco River.

Generally, and again especially among the poor, funerals are no more elaborate than other major events in life. Although friends and relatives mark death with condolences, usually few people outside the immediate family participate in the funeral itself. The dead, however, are remembered at least once a year on *El Día de Finados,* the Day of the Dead. This is the Feast of All Souls, falling on November 2.

Religion plays a small part in ordinary life in Roraima. There are churches in Bôa Vista, the capital, and a church as well as a mission school in Murusu. But for most ranchers a trip into town is difficult and time-consuming. The few roads that exist are usually impassable even on horseback during the wet season.

LAND AND ECONOMY

The territory of Roraima in northern Brazil lies along the equator. The land is partly level, partly hilly. The northwestern part, along the Venezuelan border, is mountainous. Mount Roraima, nine thousand feet in altitude, is the highest peak. In the south, along the Amazon, lie tropical rain forests. Between the rain forests and the mountains is a large area of savanna, or level grassland. Fingers of savanna also reach into highland valleys in the north. Most of Roraima's population reside on the savanna. About four-fifths of the annual rainfall of sixty or so inches falls during the wet season between April and August. The season is fairly cool but it is a highly humid period and therefore uncomfortable. Dry season daytime temperatures are

high, but relative humidity is low and nights are cool.

Ranch buildings, in Roraima are rather ordinary, except for the houses of the fairly well-to-do, which are made of brick. Most are wooden frame buildings with palm thatching for roofs.

Savanna soil is not especially fertile. Consequently the grass is low in nutritional quality. Still, it provides food for the herds of cattle that form the basis of the Roraima economy.

During the 1960s there were some 200,000 cattle in Roraima, scattered on slightly more than five hundred ranches. More than half the ranches contained fewer than 1,000 hectares, or 2,471 acres. The remainder of the ranches ranged between 1,000 and 5,000 hectares, with four containing more than 10,000. Since 80 to 100 acres are needed to graze one cow, a 1,000-hectare ranch holds only about 25 to 30 head of cattle.

Work on all but the smallest ranches is in charge of a *vaqueiro*. He is responsible for the cattle. When additional cowhands are needed, he must hire and pay for them. Since they are paid in cattle, vaqueiros frequently accumulate herds and become *fazendeiros,* or ranchers, themselves.

Ranch work is an equalizer. One cannot, for example, tell owner from vaqueiro or cowhand by the way they dress:

The everyday clothes of the rancher and the cowhand are indistinguishable, and their appearance is far from glamorous. In spite of the fact that many of the present Roraimaenses came from the northeast of Brazil, in ascending the Amazon and the Rio Branco they left behind much of *nordestino* [northeastern] custom and tradition. For example, they have discarded the traditional leather clothing which, while so essential among the thorn bushes of the *caatinga* [scrub forest], is barely necessary on the open plains of the Rio Branco. Nearly everyone on the savanna wears loose and badly fitting trousers that have baggy legs narrowed in to the ankles. Shirts tend to be equally loose-fitting and are worn outside the trousers. Most clothes are homemade; ready-to-wear shirts and trousers are worn, but are often kept for best because they are of poor quality and do not last long if submitted to the hard wear of every day. Everyone wears a hat, the usual type being of straw with a wide brim. Felt hats can also be bought in Bôa Vista, but these are usually kept for best by those who own them (mainly the richer ranchers), since they are hotter and heavier than the straw type. The hat is virtually a distinguishing mark of the cattleman; visitors from the town rarely wear them, and in a mixed working party of boatmen and cowhands [when cows go to market] it is always possible to pick out the latter by the presence of their hats. Few people wear shoes more elaborate than sandals with a thong that passes between the two biggest toes. Boots are occasionally worn, but most often by those who have lately come to be ranchers rather than by those brought up in the ranching tradition.

No additional clothes are worn for riding. A man sometimes dons a pair of leather leggings, a vestige of the full-size chaps of the northeast. Spurs are usually worn, always if cattle are to be worked; these are often strapped on to bare feet. A leather thong riding lash hangs by a loop from the right wrist. A knife of some sort, from a small sheath knife to a long machete, is always carried when leaving the vicinity of the ranch; as many people as can afford them carry revolvers, usually a .22 caliber, but occasionally a .32, .38, or even a .45. The smaller caliber is more popular because of the price and the weight of the ammunition. Marksmanship with these guns is of a low order and they are very rarely used. Sometimes as a result of boredom an old tin can is used as a target, but the only times I observed a revolver practically employed were an unsuccessful attempt to hunt a deer from horseback and the successful slaughter of a cow from point-blank range. Even if they are of little practical value, there is considerable etiquette surrounding the wearing of sidearms. No one will sit down to eat wearing a gun. Nor would one enter another's house with a gun, the normal practice being to leave it in the bunkhouse or near the door of the house. In the small cowtown of Murusu, the *delegado* (sheriff) has decreed that all visitors are to hand in their arms at the police post on arrival in town and can collect them there again on departure. The small bar and the general store in which I lived for some months had a notice to this effect on the wall. This, together with the other behavior surrounding sidearms, seems to reflect an almost conscious attempt to emulate the "Wild West" in certain areas of their lives.

Women generally wear shapeless, homemade dresses and either go barefoot or wear sandals. Some women when riding wear trousers under their dresses. "Some of the younger unmarried women of the interior," anthropologist Peter Rivière noted, "have taken to wearing slacks or Bermuda shorts; these are regarded as very dashing and have only been adopted by those who have spent some time in the city. Leaders in female fashions in the interior tend to be the young schoolmistresses who have an urban background."

DAILY AND SEASONAL WORK

The typical ranch day begins before dawn, at about 4:30 A.M., with the feeding of corraled livestock and the milking of cows. An hour later, the first *cafezinho* of the day is served. (Cafezinho is strong, black coffee.) Breakfast at seven consists of more cafezinho along with dried salt beef, milk, and *farinha*—a flour ground from manioc root—all mixed together.

The season governs daily work. Although there is a small cattle drive in the wet season, during most of that time there is little the men can do save fetch water, gather firewood, maintain corrals, and watch it rain. Once a month men ride out to check grazing cattle. One day each month, wet season or dry, is usually devoted to slaughtering a cow for food.

A brief siesta always follows the midday meal of salt beef, farinha, rice, beans, and sometimes potatoes or sweet potatoes. At about three in the afternoon the dairy cows are brought in from pasture. Women bathe in the stream—most ranches are located on one—late in the afternoon. As evening falls, men take their baths. The evening meal, much like the one at noon, comes soon after dark. At night the family listens to the daily radio broadcast of messages concerning births, deaths, anniversary congratulations, and so on. By 9 P.M. everyone is asleep in hammocks.

Roundups mark the busiest time of the year in Roraima. During the wet season roundup, cowhands pull out cattle to be sent to market. This is the time when grass is best and cattle fattest. It is also the only time the Branco is high enough for livestock to be shipped on barges to market. The barges go south down the river to the Negro, then to Manaus, where the Negro joins the Amazon.

The larger and main roundup occurs during the dry season between December and March. This is a great undertaking. It is spread over several months because ranchers cooperate to accomplish it. Together they round up the herds of one ranch, then of another. Cowboys fan out over the range to gather the cows and drive them to appropriate ranches. There they are placed in a corral. "All this," wrote Peter Rivière, "sounds far easier than it in fact is."

Indeed, the term used for roundup, *campeada,* with its connotations of military campaigns, fighting, and domination, gives some idea of the attitude toward the cattle and the nature of the roundup. Many of the cattle are half wild and run as soon as they see horses and riders approaching. In areas of rocks and bushes their speed and agility make them difficult to catch, and if they can reach a patch of real forest their safety is assured, since it is impossible to drive them from such cover. Even when cattle have been rounded into the main herd, there are usually some who are recalcitrant [stubborn] about staying with it and who make spirited attempts to escape. If a single animal is particularly stubborn, it is lassoed and held while the main herd or part of it is driven around it, whereupon it is released. Another technique used to tame a wild animal is to throw it. This is done by galloping alongside the beast, catching hold of its tail, and twisting it so that the hind legs come out of phase with the front ones and the animal falls very heavily. This sort of treatment is normally enough to take the fight out of any animal, but there are still those whose spirit is never broken. On one occasion I saw a furious cow jump an eight-foot corral fence and crash through a closed gate and a barbed wire fence in order to escape. On another occasion a wild bull jumped from a high bank into a wide, fast-flowing river and swam to safety. Often a young steer will outmaneuver and outrun the cowhands pursuing it.

Cattle rarely seem to attack horses. I saw this happen only once, when a horse was used to work cattle in a corral, which is regarded as a dangerous thing to do. Considering the nature of the work and the terrain over which it is done, injuries to men and horses are very few. Cowhands fall off their horses with relative frequency, and both horse and rider often fall while galloping on the rough and rocky ground, but such incidents rarely result in more than a few bruises and hurt pride.

Cattle are sorted and new calves branded. The cattle are vaccinated against disease, and a mixture of water, salt, and disinfectant is forced down their throats to kill parasites.

Roraima cattle are long-legged, long-horned, rangy animals of assorted colorings. They have never fetched high prices on the market, for the quality of meat is low. The high cost of transport has hindered herd improvement. Improving the quality of the cattle would not bring in enough more money to justify the extra expense. And besides, among the ranchers of Roraima, capital for such improvement is scarce.

Improved transportation facilities, however, might lead to gradual change in Roraima. For decades there has been talk of building a road between Bôa Vista in the north and Manaus on the Amazon in the south. This would be part of a major road network between Caracas, Venezuela, and Rio de Janiero. Such a transportation system would make possible the shipment of cattle by truck at any time of the year so that the Roraimaenses need no longer depend on the Rio Branco. The trip to market by truck would be speedier than by barge. The cattle would suffer less weight loss and be in better condition generally upon arrival. The demand for Roraima cattle might be increased. This could lead to herd improvement as well as to the introduction of better strains of grass. In time slaughtering facilities might be developed in Roraima, enabling its people to benefit from the sale of such by-products as hides.

Change, however, proceeds slowly. The traditional way of life in Roraima is not likely to disappear in the near future.

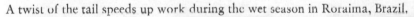

A twist of the tail speeds up work during the wet season in Roraima, Brazil.

THE PEOPLE OF SAN PEDRO, COLOMBIA

Chapter 10

San Pedro, Colombia, is a small town. It contains hardly fifteen hundred people. The town, however, is far from isolated. San Pedro is located along the main road that runs from Buenaventura on the Pacific Ocean eastward to Cali, then north along an Andes Mountain valley. San Pedro lies in a valley, between two larger towns, Tuluá to the north and Buga to the south. Wrote anthropologist Miles Richardson, who spent some time in the town:

> For those accustomed to seeing only two types of Spanish Americans, the peasant and the aristocrat, San Pedro is a surprise. San Pedro functions, and Sanpedranos act, like Mainstreet and Mainstreeters. San Pedro is neither a quaint peasant community, nor a glittering urban complex; it is simply a town, and its people, ordinary townspeople.

> As a place, San Pedro is the political, educational, medical, religious, recreational, and to a diminishing degree, the market center of the rural area surrounding it. The location of these activities within San Pedro makes it structurally more complex than a hamlet or a village. The smallness in scale of these enterprises and the informality in which they are carried out separates San Pedro from a city. In the sense that it is neither village nor city, San Pedro resembles the North American rural town. Furthermore, just as rural towns in the United States are losing economic control of their clientele, so the merchants of San Pedro are hard pressed to meet the cheaper prices and larger ranges of goods available in city stores.

Like all traditional Latin American communities, San Pedro is built around a plaza, a central square. The church, the priest's house, and the parish hall occupy one corner and about half of one side of the square. Government buildings, residences, bars, and a few stores make up the remainder of the buildings. The town has two elementary schools. The boys' school is found just off the main highway. The girls' school lies on the other side of town, about a block from the plaza. Near the boys' school, along the highway, there is a cigar factory. There are other smaller cigar factories within the town. Cigar making is an important industry in San Pedro.

There is no hospital in San Pedro, but there is one in Buga, easily reached by jeep or pickup truck. An intern commutes regularly from Buga to attend patients in a clinic that serves workers such as those in the cigar factories

Opposite: Peruvian businessmen. An air of courtly reserve known as *dignidad* is typical of officials and businessmen throughout Latin America.

and a health station that cares for the remainder of the population.

The houses in San Pedro are as traditional as the town itself. One enters directly from the street into a parlorlike room. Crossing that room, through another door one comes to a patio, either fenced or walled. Other rooms are arranged on either side of this patio.

As to the people of San Pedro, the Sanpedranos:

There is Don Hernán, the *alcalde* [mayor]. A mixture of informality and restraint, he moves easily through the town. He stops to give a kid a few centavos for a coke; he goes into *El Bar Central* for a beer but never gets visibly drunk. He is *una persona muy formal,* "a very formal person," friendly, kind, but correct. In his own words, he is the father of San Pedro; he speaks to the governor of the Valle about the needs of his town and *municipio*. An owner of a sizeable area of land in the *municipio,* he lives immediately outside of town. Yet he and his wife feel middle class, and they talk about moving into Buga, his birthplace. He launched a vigorous compaign to purchase a small, waist-high refrigerator, one of the few in town, that the anthropologist had bought in a used appliance store in Tuluá. Don Hernán, by overpowering the owner with free drinks and demanding pleas that friends sell cheaper to each other, defeated his competitor, the *municipio* judge. Before the sale was finalized his wife took her friends to the owner's house to hear their admiring comments about her useful adornment.

There is Pedro, who worked for a while in a cigar factory in a position that was a strange combination of flunky and foreman. Before he left to work in a leather shop in Tuluá, Pedro liked to talk about philosophy and culture, about [former United States Vice-President] Henry Wallace's trip to Colombia and about the singing of Nelson Eddy [a movie star]. Pedro's drinking buddy, who does not care for abstract discussions, is Ramón, the furniture maker. Ramón keeps magazine pictures of furniture styles under his bed and pulls them out to show to his prospective customers. Despite the choice that he offers, he does not seem to be able to escape from producing a monumental style he calls Louis XV [after a French king of the eighteenth century]. An unexpected customer or two allowed him to expand into the bar business, but Pedro, Ramón, and other friends drank up both profit and credit, so he, his wife, and child left town one quiet night.

Don Carlos, the tailor, came from Cali, searching, as did Ramón, for a place without competition. Don Carlos, however, is like the *alcalde;* he is a formal person, entitled to respect. When he talks about Spanish, the language of love, or about English, the language of Shakespeare, people listen —even and especially teenage boys. . . .

Chucho is a prosperous native son of San Pedro. He owns one of the largest cigar factories in San Pedro and has recently expanded into raising chickens. During the day he strolls about in a half-opened sport shirt. At night he sits in the park quietly explaining to his Catholic friends the profundities [deep insights] of their faith, how the faith prohibits them from killing and how it instructs them to help their neighbors. He rarely drinks and never goes to church. Prosperous, correct, and formal, Chucho is only occasionally called Don. Perhaps it is because Chucho is a nickname for Jesús and "Don Chucho" sounds a little silly, or perhaps it is due to his youth and his life as a hometown boy. . . .

Don Guido, the school director, is an

Ospiña. The Ospiñas, according to Don Guido, came from Spain to Colombia some two hundred years ago. They have never mixed with Indians and prefer to marry members of another pure family, the Tascóns. Don Guido, however, found an *antioqueña* [a native woman from Antioquia, a region to the north] more to his liking. Commenting not so much about his own children but about children in general, he says that they no longer believe in witches or *duendes* (malicious, elflike creatures). In fact they do not even believe in the police. The children of today do not respect authority, either public or parental, as they did in his youth. The flaunting of authority is the result of modern times a modernity characterized by soft drink and easy virtue.

MARRIAGE

The men of San Pedro generally accept the Latin American tradition of male supremacy. Macho is highly valued and much admired. Still, a husband does not necessarily run a Sanpedrano family, as Richardson noted:

Once Sunday afternoon, Don Carlos, Pedro, and Ramón were talking about the way they run their families. Ramón had just finished saying that the man has the right to expect his wife to obey him. Carlos added, "I know of a case where the woman is of a higher class than her husband, and because she has more money, she can dominate the man. But I agree with you. When the man and the woman are of the same class, then he dominates the woman. Like in my family."

Just then Don Carlos' wife appeared at the door. "Carlos," she said, "the goats need milking." With neither a word nor glance, Don Carlos rose and left.

To enter into marriage, a Sanpedrano couple

might simply decide to live together. A few do. Or a couple might be married in a civil ceremony. Very few do this. Most are married in the Catholic church.

EARNING A LIVING

Although about a quarter of Sanpedrano families depend to some extent on farming for a living, all Sanpedranos consider themselves city dwellers. Child rearing practices there are much the same as in any urban area where children are not economically useful, as they are in a strictly rural community. Girls learn household tasks, more as a matter of course than as a conscious preparation for marriage. Boys sometimes follow their fathers' footsteps in a trade such as tailoring. Most children receive some schooling. Some go on to the six-year secondary school in Buga or Tuluá. Most remain with their families until marriage. And, as adults, most work for wages.

The cigar factories provide employment for some fifty or more Sanpedrano men and women. Chicken raising is another income-producing occupation. A few Sanpedranos are local government officials. Others are tailors or barbers, or they run stores or bars. San Pedro itself is no longer important as a market center. Those with surplus maize or with chickens to sell frequently transport their produce to Tuluá. Locally grown tobacco, of course, finds a ready market in the cigar-making factories of San Pedro.

Two types of factories produce cigars. There are the three small, part-time operations like that of Climaco. He sets up his production line of two or three people in a spare room of his house when he has accumulated sufficient leaves. Climaco's partner, Chucho, and Mario Tascón operate the two much larger, full-time factories, which together employ fifty-seven workers.

Chucho worked in Mario's factory until he had learned the process and then set up his own factory. On the street in front of his house, he nearly always has drying mats covered with chopped tobacco leaves, and inside along the sheltered sides of the patio, he has several production lines going simultaneously. Making a cigar is a rapid affair once men have chopped the leaves into bits with their machetes. One person molds the bits into the body of the cigar, and another compresses the body and covers it with a single leaf. This final stage calls for the skilled manipulation of small hand rollers, and consequently the operator receives more money. Chucho pays his workers, not by the hour, but by the number of cigars they make in a day. Before he can ship the cigars to be sold in Cali, he also has to pay a governmental tax graded according to the quality of the cigar. His best cigar, The Queen, sells for 15 centavos (about 1.5 cents), and on these cigars he is taxed 35 pesos ($3.50) per thousand. Chucho would like to buy machines and reduce his production expenses, but he says he cannot because the Colombian government prohibits the importation of cigar machines.

Mario Tascón lives in Tuluá, where he has other business interests, and daily travels to his San Pedro cigar factory, which occupies a house located on the outskirts of town. He employs fewer people, twenty-two, than does Chucho but produces a better quality cigar from tobacco imported from a city in northern Colombia, Barranquilla. His best cigar is a rum crook, La Cigalia, which sells for 25 centavos. Mario has a machine to render the leaves into bits, but the rest of the process is hand labor, which, according to Mario, makes a better cigar. In the familiar manner of the businessman, he bemoans the high governmental tax, because it keeps him from paying a

higher salary to his workers. The low salary makes it difficult to get help.

The workers in the two large cigar factories are among the elite of the town laborers. They are participants in the national social security plan which guarantees them medical care, and their fairly steady income receives a yearly boost with a bonus at Christmas. Work in the factories is one of the few legitimate jobs that a San Pedro woman can hold outside of her house. Perhaps nearly half of the total work force in the two factories are women, and fourteen female heads of families, as contrasted to only nine male heads, find employment in the factories.

Señor José Rafael Rojas is the epitome [perfect example] of a small town captain of industry and the most representative of San Pedro's businessmen. He is the owner of Indusrojas, an industry for producing billiard cues. Throughout Colombia men amuse themselves in bars playing billiards, and settlements much smaller than San Pedro have at least one table. Señor Rojas has effectively tied himself into this immense market. His factory occupies all of the patio of his house, and cue sticks overflow into the bedrooms. All steps in making the cues, except painting, are mechanized. Electric powered saws reduce the wood brought from Tuluá into long rectangular strips, and lathes turn the strips into cues.

Don José, in his own way, confronts the paradoxes that plague a developing country. In order to diversify its economy, Colombia needs to industrialize; it has to protect native industrialists from foreign competition. The things that it protects, the tips of cues and sandpaper, Don José needs. He can buy tips and paper made in Colombia, but according to him, they are not any good. These limitations are a constant irritation to him. "I understand," he says, "that Colombia has to produce its own goods, but what is being produced now is inferior. Of course in the future Colombia will manufacture first-class material, but now, here am I, trying to make a good cue with tips that break and sandpaper that tears."

A native of San Pedro, Señor Rojas is a bustling, talkative person, who prides himself as a self-made man. He employs two or three workers, but exclaims, "In this house everyone works! The smallest child can carry a stick, from here to there. Like the capitalists in the United States and in Japan, I built my factory up from nothing. I taught myself how to make cues, and it took me three days to make my first cue. When I started, all the capital that I had was one peso and twenty centavos. Now my factory turns out many sticks in one day, and I am worth several thousand pesos."

THE WORLD OF GOVERNMENT AND POLITICS

As a political unit, San Pedro is the center of a municipio, a district that takes in the town along with nearby villages and hamlets. San Pedro government officials are responsible to officials at Cali, the department (state) capital. They in turn are responsible to officials in the nation's capital, Bogotá. The president of Colombia appoints department governors, who in turn appoint municipio alcaldes—mayors—for one-year terms. The alcalde is always selected from the majority party in the municipio, which in the case of San Pedro is the Liberal party.

The alcalde administers laws. He occasionally joins the municipio judge to consider such minor disputes as those concerning property rights. He also acts as police chief or sheriff.

Perhaps Don Hernán's most important job is to let the government in Cali know the needs of his people, that his *municipio* needs roads into the mountains and that the town must have secondary schools to avoid the expense of sending children to Buga or to Tuluá. In expressing these needs, Don Hernán self-consciously adopts the posture of a father looking after his children. He explains that he is like a family head demanding order and harmony in his household. The ordinary person is one without influence and without protection against the rapacious [greedy] politicians. For his children's sake, Don Hernán puts on his armor of wisdom and lays on his influence among the bureaucratic dragons in Cali.

An elected council of eight members assists the alcalde. Council members, who serve two-year terms, are equally divided between Liberals and Conservatives. Meeting twice a year, the council fixes tax rates, lets contracts for public works, and generally sees after municipio needs. Taxes are levied mainly on businesses, property, and livestock.

Finally, there is a judge appointed by the district court at Buga. He settles land and marital disputes and problems concerning inheritance, and hears cases involving petty theft. The judge can levy fines and hand out short-term jail sentences.

Sanpedranos, like Latin Americans generally, take their politics seriously. Party membership is inherited. Children absorb their parents' political points of view. To a certain extent, the differences between Conservatives and Liberals are much the same as they were in the nineteenth century. The Conservative party is the party of the landed elite; the Liberal, that of mestizos and intellectuals. Sanpedranos tend to make politics a personal thing, giving their support not so much to party as to individual leaders within a party. While they possess intense feelings about politics, Sanpedranos dislike *políticos,* those who want only to get elected and never keep their campaign promises.

FIESTAS, RELIGIOUS AND SECULAR

Religion is also a serious matter among Sanpedranos. Nearly all are faithful Catholics. Even those skeptical about the church's role in business and political affairs and indifferent about attending mass consider themselves Catholics from birth to death.

Saints' days are regularly celebrated, and Christmas in San Pedro is a particularly festive occasion. The season begins on December 15. Traditionally it is celebrated each night by a different group of Sanpedranos. On one night, unmarried women or *señoritas* are the center of attention:

The *señoritas,* following their mass, gather in front of the church. On the church steps are the members of the *municipio* band that the *señoritas* have hired. The band launches into a number, and a man lights the first fireworks of the night. These are large rockets which zoom up just above the houses and explode with a really satisfying noise. It is part of their prerogative, that on this special night, the *señoritas* can hunt for *aguinaldos* [Christmas gifts]. The *señorita* approaches a person, a boy usually, and shouts out a formula, such as *pajita emboca* (straw-in-mouth). The person sticks out his tongue and on it is a straw. If he does not have a straw, he has to give the girl a present.

The band plays, the rockets explode, and the *señoritas* chase people around the park. Someone sets fire to a cloth ball saturated [thoroughly soaked] with kerosene. Small boys swarm around him and start kicking the burning ball across the plaza. Many of the boys are barefooted, but they kick away with enthusiasm. If the ball rolls among the members of the band, so much the better. One man, crossing the plaza on his way home, has to hurry to get out of the way of the ball and its tail of small boys. He grumbles as he reaches the safety of his house, "Someone is going to get hurt with that ball." In *El Bar Central* men continue their nightly game of billiards and occasionally look up from their beer to see what is happening. Women, sitting in front of their houses as they have done on every other night, try to keep up their conversation about what has occurred during the day. The ball disintegrates into bits of cloth, the band breaks up, and by nine o'clock, the *señoritas* leave the park for their homes.

Sanpedranos decorate their houses. No one any longer builds a manger scene. Everyone buys cardboard models from dime stores in Tuluá. Store and bar owners place models on a counter. A few families have Christmas trees. They use a deciduous bush stripped of leaves and bark, and decorate it with imitation snow. Instead of Santa Claus, Sanpedrano children believe in *El Niño de Díos,* the Christ Child, who brings them gifts on Christmas Eve. Midnight mass—"the mass of the rooster"—follows the Christ Child's visit.

Sanpedranos exchange Christmas cards. Christmas Day itself is a family day, when sons and daughters who are away return. *El Día de los Inocentes,* marking the day King Herod had children killed in a vain attempt to destroy the Christ Child, is celebrated December 28. Sanpedranos observe this day by playing jokes on one another. It is their version of April Fool's Day. The end of December is a time of visiting and exchanging drinks. Midnight mass on New Year's Eve is followed by visits to the graves of relatives. *El Día de los Reyes*—commemorating the day the three kings paid homage to the Christ Child—falls on January 6. This ends the Christmas season.

During the Easter season, Sanpedranos, like Latin Americans generally, place greater emphasis on the crucifixion than on the resurrection. Chucho explained why:

"No, this is not fatalism," insisted Chucho. "It is realism. Christ died so that we too could learn how to suffer and how to die. To live is to die. It is part of the human tragedy. Through his actions, Christ teaches us this tragedy and how we must face death."

"When Jesus was on his way to the cross, would not it have been better if he had fought against his persecutors?"

"No. He wanted to set an example. He wanted to show us how to suffer patiently, how to accept death with tranquility. Today, humans do not suffer correctly or formally. They do not patiently await the outcome. They fight against death. This is because they do not have the image of Christ in their minds. Because we are humans, we cannot die in the manner of Christ, who was God. But we must try. If God suffered patiently, then surely we must do likewise. We must try to conform to death. This is the reason why Holy Friday is more important than Resurrection Sunday."

Besides religious festivals, Sanpedranos occasionally stage a community celebration. One year, for example, they elected a queen of the chicken industry. As part of the three-day celebration in her honor, they staged a bullfight, a favorite Colombian sport. No one could afford real bulls, of course, but those who arranged the events rented a steer and a cow from a nearby farmer. Men built a small stadium out of split bamboo and young boys acted the parts of *toreros,* or bullfighters.

Preparations were completed; the day of the fight arrived. After purchasing their tickets, the spectators cautiously mounted the rickety steps and gingerly sat down on the benches which immediately sagged a dangerous inch or two. Someone put fight music on a phonograph, and with the sounds of a *paso doble* [a marching tune] blaring out, the two boys marched the few steps from the entrance to the center of the arena. While they were doffing their caps to the crowd, a young friend rushed out with his Brownie camera and took their picture. Then the "bulls" were let in. The first one, a young steer, despite his ears being split to make him vicious, charged only once or twice. Although the boys seemed content with the steer's performance, the audience was not, and two or three men lit newspapers and dropped the burning paper on the steer's back. However, the steer refused to charge and was turned out, and the cow was let in. She immediately knocked one boy down and ran the other behind his bamboo barricade. This episode completely satisfied the boys' quest for valor and glory, and despite the abuse that the audience hurled at them, they refused to fight. Several men from the crowd impatiently jumped down into the ring and using their shirts as capes, provoked several rushes from the cow. She soon became exhausted, and although her slit ears were pulled, her tail twisted, and burning paper thrown on her, she could not gather strength to charge. So ended the bullfight; an ancient ritual that pits man against beast and in the process tears away man's pretentions and allows him to gaze upon his true self.

The tradition of the bullfight is one of the common bonds between the townspeople of San Pedro and the people of the city. Unlike a peasant village, San Pedro is closely tied through such traditions, through its government, and through religion to larger communities and to the nation.

But San Pedro is a poor town. And the spectacle of the bullfight in San Pedro is "made sadly comic by poverty."

In 1961, after several years of planning, the government of Venezuela founded a new industrial center in the country's interior. The center was developed in the city of Guayana, where the Caroní River joins the Orinoco. The government built a steel mill, a dam, and an electric power plant. More industrialization was planned. Two mining companies, both owned by United States steel companies, had headquarters there. At the time, about 40,000 people lived in Guayana. Planners expected a population of some 250,000 in about ten years. By 1986, the population had reached 442,000 and was climbing rapidly. Wrote an observer about the city:

It is eight degrees off the equator and nearly at sea level; the sky seems extraordinarily wide and clear and pours down light and heat. The wide Orinoco River and the more rocky Caroní, which rushes from the south to fall over a magnificent waterfall and run into the Orinoco at the city site, interrupt but do not temper the land. Under that wide sky's bowl of light the new roads and new concrete buildings—rows of developer houses, apartment buildings, commercial structures—seem to erupt from the dust-dry earth which bulldozers have scraped clear of vegetation. Elsewhere, the improvised housing of the poor, of sheet aluminum or pressed-board, looks as if it had been thrown together by a hurricane. It is a city of bulldozers, of engineers who wear boots and dungarees and carry shiny briefcases, of noisy bars and holes in the streets, and of new traffic interchanges. It is a city of building and of disorderly entrepreneurship [the organizing of business enterprises]. It is a city which lives in the future.

Oil discoveries in Venezuela early in the twentieth century stimulated continuing change in that country. By 1929 Venezuelan oil wells, mostly owned by foreign companies, made Venezuela second in production only to the United States. The exploitation of oil resources led eventually to the development of manufacturing and to urbanization. In the mid-1930s Venezuela was two-thirds rural. By the 1960s it was two-thirds urban. Fewer and fewer Venezuelans lived in the state in which they had been born. Many continued to leave the countryside to reside and work in such cities as Guayana. And many lived in *barrios,* or communities, such as La Laja.

In the early 1960s La Laja was three blocks of small, one-story houses, most constructed of cinder block, some of wood. The barrio held 490 people, 229 of them children under

Opposite: Favelas or shanty towns crowd the surrounding hillsides and mar the splendor of Rio de Janeiro, Brazil. Sugar Loaf Mountain rises in the background.

thirteen. Only 9 of the La Laja adults had been born in Guayana. Most newcomers to La Laja came from towns along the Orinoco. Some came from rural areas.

GOING TO SCHOOL

The barrio has its own school, a modern building that houses grades one to four. Some children go to a mining company school. A few attend Catholic or Protestant schools. Wrote anthropologist Lisa Redfield Peattie, who lived in La Laja for many months:

For the families of La Laja, sending children to school does not involve a choice between education and immediate income as it does in some countries, for the ways in which children can earn money are extremely limited. But it is not without appreciable [significant] economic costs. There is the cost of the school uniforms and shoes, and a cost, in soap and labor at least, of laundry; for while a dirty dress is acceptable for playing in the barrio, it is not so for attendance at school. For those who go to school out of walking distance, there is the bus fare. Finally, but not least, there is the cost of pencils, papers, and books, since schools neither issue books nor have libraries. Children whose parents work for the two American mining companies have their school supplies paid for by the company, but for other families the cost of books may mean a choice between non-attendance and attending school without books.

Children start school at ages which vary considerably, according to the [particular demands arising from] their parents' mobility and circumstances at various times. Furthermore, they may drop out for con-

siderable periods. In addition, the rate of repetitions in Venezuelan primary schools is, for a number of reasons, extremely high. There is, as a result, much less correlation between grade level and age than in North American schools. Children in one grade may differ over five years in age. I found a number of cases like that in which a thirteen-year-old and her eight-year-old sister were together in second grade.

In addition to the three R's, primary schools present material on personal health and hygiene, plants and animals, and on the geography and history of Venezuela, focusing very heavily on Simón Bolívar and the period of the Wars of Independence. Teaching methods emphasize rote repetition and writing from dictation and copying, and stick very closely to texts. I was present at a sixth-grade lesson on economic development in Venezuela, one which had obviously been very thoroughly prepared by a confident-appearing teacher. It treated Venezuela's economic possibilities almost exclusively in terms of minable resources such as gold and diamonds, making almost no reference to development of manufacturing. Hydroelectric power was not mentioned. No reference was made to the steel mill or the Guayana development program. The mastery of both skills and "material" thus appears as a rather specialized undertaking, not connected with the experiences of everyday life. . . .

One goes to school in a clean dress not just to learn things, but also to become an educated person. In a country like Venezuela, which until rather recently has had a highly stratified class order with formal education associated with upper-class status, this is an exciting idea. To be educated is not just to have information and be able to practice skills; it is to conceive of oneself differently.

Schooling brings change. And so do other avenues of communication. Wrote anthropologist Peattie:

> Mass communications also, of course, bring in the new. Jukebox and radio teach new songs; cinema, magazine, and newspaper depict new styles of dress and makeup, new dances, new sorts of behavior. Even the goods sold in the market are a kind of information on and enticement [temptation] to new styles of consumption and of self-presentation. This process has gone very far among the Venezuelan *clase obrero* [working class]. Oil prosperity and the spread of mass communications have transmitted mass market consumption styles far into the rural areas which lie beyond the cities. It is not remarkable, then, that in La Laja mass communication "styling" dominates many aspects of life. Girls do their hair in roller hairdos in imitation of the latest fashion in Caracas or New York. Their dresses also follow the fashion to the best of their ability. The kitchen at the back of the house is likely to be dirty and untidy, lacking the "presentation" aspects so important to the North American middle class, but perhaps this is just because the housewives of La Laja haven't heard *that* news yet; the living room is almost sure to feature plastic upholstered furniture, a coffee table, plastic flowers and ornaments. There is, then, a revolution in styling, in self-presentation, going on, stimulated and directed by the spread of mass communications and of the cash economy.

THE ECONOMY AND THE FAMILY

Not everyone in Barrio La Laja knows everyone else. This is one thing that makes La Laja different from a rural community. Families move in and out. Nearly all have interests and social connections outside the barrio. Still, contrary to what frequently occurs in cities, kinship ties in La Laja remain fairly strong. In the 1960s, two-thirds of the families had some kinship connection—through uncles, aunts, nephews, nieces, and so on—with at least one other family. This makes for a certain amount of stability. It serves to prop up a family or an individual in times of stress, such as periods of unemployment. Barrio residents also have kinship ties with families in other parts of the city. These are loose, however, for communication is difficult. There are no telephones, and bus rides can be long and expensive.

Other aspects of city life place stress on individuals and families. Traditionally, a young man asks his intended wife's parents for permission to marry her. Generally, this is not the case in La Laja. It is not uncommon for a girl simply to "go off" with a man. They may marry later, they may not. Church weddings are uncommon. People say it is too expensive. Many women forego a church wedding because, except under very special circumstances, the Catholic church forbids divorce. A couple can survive even if their parents disapprove of their marriage or their living together. Economically the two do not need the family.

Economically they do not need each other either. Most employed persons of Barrio La Laja are equipped for only low-paying unskilled jobs. But usually, in a boomtown situation, one can find something to do in order to get by. It is more difficult for women to find employment. Even so, a number of barrio families are headed and supported by women. The woman is widowed, or the man left her, or she left him. On the whole, in the barrio marriage is a rather unstable institution.

And so is religion. A number of residents of La Laja are Protestants. The remainder are Catholics only in the barest form. They are baptized and buried in the church, and they celebrate first communion. But that is about the extent of it. Even extreme unction—last rites for the dying—is not a common practice.

Religious shrines and pictures are absent from La Laja houses.

COMMUNITY ACTION

La Laja residents have been slow to develop community cohesion and the kind of informal social control found in well-established and especially rural communities. People tend to look to themselves and to their families, not to the community as a whole. The highly personalized society of La Laja, Peattie says, is "too loosely meshed to cage anyone." The group rarely tries to control a person who won't cooperate or who annoys others. The people who do occasion-ally try to stop someone from being disruptive usually wind up being criticized themselves. The ideal in the barrio is to be a "family of respect" that "doesn't get involved" in quarrels with the neighbors. The ideal is not easy to achieve.

Certain social techniques have been developed to make this easier. One is that of using children as intermediaries. That it is always a child who comes to borrow a lime or an egg . . . might be seen as a particular instance of the general practice of having children run errands at the store. But the fact that a child is sent to ask a favor—a car ride to town for a sick family member, for example, or, bearing a small closely folded note, to ask for a loan of money— seems to be a way of avoiding either an embarrassing refusal or direct hostility. Another technique is the general practice, at least by parents who take the child-rearing role seriously, of immediately disciplining a child seen annoying a neighbor.

La Laja residents hate to criticize a neighbor to his face, no matter how annoying his behavior might be. For instance, the La Laja barrio council held a long discussion about the pig problem. Five of the barrio families kept pigs. Rather than pen the animals up, these families allowed the pigs to wander loose, scavenging as much of their food as they could. A good deal of dirt and disorder resulted. The barrio leaders talked of making a complaint to the police or to the city authorities in charge of sanitation. When an outsider suggested that instead they talk directly to the families and ask them to pen up their pigs, the council refused to consider such action. Peattie gives several other examples that illustrate how little the community has generally done to control troublemakers or those who are uncooperative.

A squealing pig on its way to market in the Barrio La Laja, Guayana, Venezuela.

When a considerable group of men were working as unpaid volunteers to finish the barrio's water line, there were other men in the barrio who took no hand in the work. Some sat playing cards in plain sight of a team working away in the hot sun. They did not appear ill at ease in the situation, nor was any attempt made, that I could see, to sanction [punish] them for their non-participation, beyond a friendly invitation to join the job.

One man in the barrio, otherwise liked and respected, formed the habit of playing his radio at top volume every morning from about 5:00 A.M. until he left for work at twenty minutes to six. . . . Similarly, when the bar played music late at night and again early in the morning, and when one evening a group of people experimented with a loudspeaker emitting ear-splitting racket into the street, no one felt it proper to object (until, finally, I did—in the last case—and had my plea immediately and courteously heeded).

As a result, when people do finally decide to "involve themselves" in quarrels with their neighbors, they frequently call in the police. During her first year of residence in the barrio, anthropologist Peattie recalls five cases in which the police were called. Only one of these involved someone from outside the barrio, a person caught burglarizing a house. The other cases all involved barrio residents, mostly caught up in minor family quarrels.

Still, Peattie saw in the development of the barrio council a groping towards a better way of handling community problems. And the council, along with some outside agencies, did make some progress.

Petitions were sent in asking that the barrio get electricity, and after some negotiation the national electrification agency brought in electricity. There were a number of community parties—refreshments, sack races, climbing the greased pole, toys for children. Adult education classes were held in the schoolhouse at night for some months. Trees were planted in the open spaces, tended, and watered. A vacant lot was converted into a children's playground by planting trees and constructing two merry-go-rounds out of large scavenged wheels set in cement.

Also, a cement-block building was constructed so that La Laja's fifty or so children could qualify for a free meal program offered by the state.

It is in the cities, of course, where one sees most of the change that is occurring in Latin America, changes in attitudes, life-styles, and —especially—in expectations. Those who obtain jobs in cities gain a little. They see about them people who have more. These are not necessarily aristocrats living on inherited wealth. Mostly they are middle class people living on a higher scale than the residents of the barrios. People who have taken a step or two up the economic ladder wish to continue moving upward. They want their children, especially, to enjoy a better life. Once visions of possible improvement are opened, there is no point at which the process can be stopped. Never can there be a return to an older way of life. Opportunities must continue to open. And providing those opportunities is perhaps the most serious problem many Latin American countries face. Anthropologist Peattie concluded her study of Barrio La Laja with this observation:

Venezuela has the capital resources and the relatively open social structures to do . . . what few other countries can do. But in that very set of advantages is also a possible source of danger. A country like Venezuela lives in hope and optimism, but also in jeopardy. . . . It can no more stop or go backward than can a boy going downhill on a bicycle with his feet on the handlebars.

The young people of La Laja are growing up in a world of schools and newspapers and movies, hair curlers, automobiles, and transistor radios. One can imagine them becoming many sorts of people, but it is not possible to conceive of them becoming *campesinos* [peasants] like their grandparents. They are committed to the world of which those things are a part. Development has to create a society with places for them, or run the risk that, finding none, they will explode the society which has failed their very high expectations. . . .

In any case, planned or unplanned, life in La Laja is part of a historic transformation. The intellectuals call it "economic development," but the people of La Laja may be on the right track when they speak of making the future, not with that dry technicians' phrase, but as *"haciendo patria"* (nation-making) and *"haciendo pueblo"* (making a people).

CAROLINA MARIA DE JESUS

Despite the fact that Guayana is a bustling, rapidly growing city, unemployment exists among residents of La Laja. At times it runs as high as 25 percent. Frequently those temporarily without income receive help from relatives. But there are many people in Latin America, individuals and families, who are strictly on their own. They are without employment or much hope of it, living only from day to day. These are the people who exist, as anthropologist Oscar Lewis put it, in "the culture of poverty." The classic example of a member of this culture is Carolina Maria de Jesus, a black Brazilian who as a child received sufficient education to learn to read and write. Using old notebooks she scavenged out of garbage cans, Carolina Maria de Jesus kept diaries.

Carolina Maria de Jesus was a *favelada*, a resident of a *favela*, or slum, in São Paulo, Brazil. Born in 1913 in the town of Sacramento in Brazil's interior, Carolina got through the second grade. Then her mother took a job on a farm and Carolina's schooling ended. Later she and her mother moved to Franca, near São Paulo. When Carolina was about sixteen, they separated.

Carolina worked at whatever job she could find—in a hospital performing menial tasks, cleaning hotel rooms, as a maid for a white family in São Paulo. She had an affair with a Portuguese sailor, who deserted her before the birth of her first child, a son. To support herself and the baby, Carolina collected scrap paper from garbage and trash heaps and sold it. On a good day she took in twenty to twenty-five cents. Another son was born, later a daughter. The family lived in a shack in the favela. Their home was made of old boards with flattened tin cans and cardboard for a roof. When it rained, the roof leaked. Stormy or clear, there were always rats and foul odors. And there was always hunger, an enemy with whom favelados must grapple every day, 365 days a year. Excerpts from the diaries of Carolina Maria de Jesus, which were published as *Child of the Dark,* provide vivid glimpses of favela life, a life of poverty.

July 15, 1955. The birthday of my daughter Vera Eunice. I wanted to buy a pair of shoes for her, but the price of food keeps us from realizing our desires. Actually we are slaves to the cost of living. I found a pair of shoes in the garbage, washed them, and patched them for her to wear.

I didn't have one cent to buy bread. So I washed three bottles and traded them to Arnaldo. He kept the bottles and gave me bread. Then I went to sell my paper. I received 65 cruzeiros [one cruzeiro was then worth about one fourth of a cent]. I spent 20 cruzeiros for meat. I got one kilo [about 2.2 pounds] of ham and one kilo of sugar and spent six cruzeiros on cheese. And the money was gone. . . .

July 16. I got up and obeyed Vera Eunice [who had told her to get some water]. I went to get the water. I made coffee. I told the children that I didn't have any bread, that they would have to drink their coffee plain and eat meat with *farinha* [manioc flour]. I was feeling ill and decided to cure myself. I stuck my finger down my throat twice, vomited, and knew I was under the evil eye. The upset feeling left and I went to Senhor Manuel, carrying some cans to sell. Everything that I find in the garbage I sell. He gave me 13 cruzeiros. I kept thinking that I had to buy bread, soap, and milk for Vera Eunice. The 13 cruzeiros wouldn't make it. I returned home, or rather to my shack, nervous and exhausted. I thought of the worrisome life that I led. Carrying paper, washing clothes for the children, staying in the street all day long. Yet I'm always lacking things, Vera doesn't have shoes and she doesn't like to go barefoot. For at least two years I've wanted to buy a meat grinder. And a sewing machine. . . .

Then came the fishmonger Senhor Antonio Lira and he gave me some fish. I started preparing lunch. The women went away, leaving me in peace for today. They

Ramshackle towns of tin, cardboard, and packing material spring up as the poor of Latin America crowd to the cities.

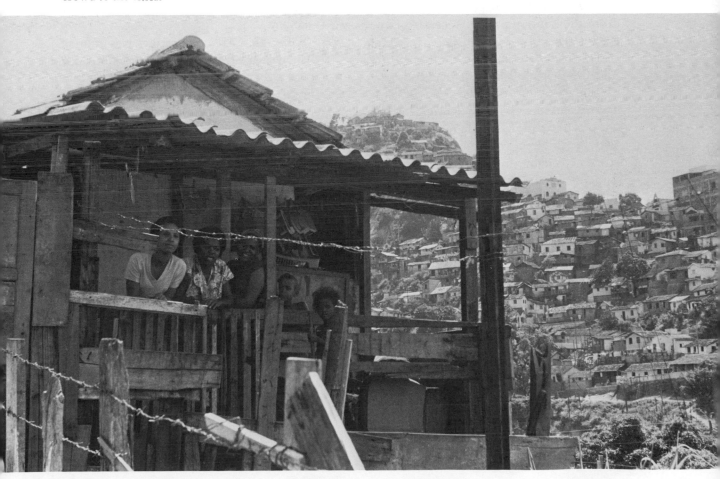

had put on their show [arguing about her children]. . . . All children throw stones, but my boys are the scapegoats. They gossip that I'm not married, but I'm happier than they are. They have husbands but they are forced to beg. They are supported by charity organizations.

My kids are not kept alive by the church's bread. I take on all kinds of work to keep them. And those women have to beg or even steal. At night when they are begging I peacefully sit in my shack listening to Viennese waltzes. While their husbands break the boards of the shack, I and my children sleep peacefully. I don't envy the married women of the favelas who lead lives like Indian slaves. . . .

I went to collect paper and stayed away from the house an hour. When I returned I saw several people at the river bank. There was a man unconscious from alcohol and the worthless men of the favela were cleaning out his pockets. They stole his money and tore up his documents. . . .

Sometimes I turn on the radio and dance with the children; we pretend we're boxing. Today I bought candy for them. I gave each one a piece and felt them looking at me a bit differently. My João said:

"What a good mother!" . . .

I finished breakfast and I washed the dishes. Then I went to wash clothes. I don't have a man at home. There is just me and my children, so I can't relax. My dream is to be very clean, to wear expensive clothes and live in a comfortable house, but it's not possible. I am not unhappy with the work I do. I am used to being dirty. I've carried paper for eight years. What disgusts me is that I must live in a favela. . . .

I was horrified! Someone burned five sacks of my paper. Dona Elvira's granddaughter, who has two girls and doesn't want any more children because her husband earns very little, said:

"We saw the smoke. And besides you put the sacks there in the street. Hide them where no one can see them." *Favelados* live by robbing from one another. . . .

My advice to would-be politicians is that people do not tolerate hunger. It's necessary to know hunger to know how to describe it. . . . Brazil needs to be led by a person who has known hunger. Hunger is also a teacher. . . .

Yesterday I got half a pig's head at the slaughterhouse. We ate the meat and saved the bones. Today I put the bones on to boil and into the broth I put some potatoes. My children are always hungry. When they are starving they aren't so fussy about what they eat. . . .

May 13, 1958. At dawn it was raining. Today is a nice day for me, it's the anniversary of the Abolition. The day we celebrate the freeing of the slaves. In the jails the Negroes were the scapegoats. But now the whites are more educated and don't treat us any more with contempt. May God enlighten the whites so that the Negroes may have a happier life.

It continued to rain and I only have beans and salt. The rain is strong but even so I sent the boys to school. I'm writing until the rain goes away so I can go to Senhor Manuel and sell scrap. With that money I'm going to buy rice and sausage. The rain has stopped for a while. I'm going out.

I feel so sorry for my children. When they see the things to eat that I come home with they shout:

"Viva Mama!"

Their outbursts please me. But I've lost the habit of smiling. Ten minutes later they want more food. I sent João to ask Dona Ida for pork fat. She didn't have any. . . .

It rained and got colder. Winter had arrived and in winter people eat more. Vera asked for food, and I didn't have any. It was the same old show. I had two cruzeiros and wanted to buy a little flour to make a *virado* [a dish made with black beans, manioc flour, pork, and eggs]. I went to ask Dona Alice for a little pork. She gave me pork and rice. It was 9 at night when we ate.

And that is the way on May 13, 1958 I fought against the real slavery—hunger! . . .

The neighbors in the brick houses near by have signed a petition to get rid of the *favelados*. But they won't get their way. The neighbors in the brick houses say:

"The politicians protect the *favelados*."

Who protects us are the public and the Order of St. Vincent Church. The politicians only show up here during election campaigns. Senhor Candido Sampaio, when he was city councilman in 1953, spent his Sundays here in the favela. He was so nice. He drank our coffee, drinking right out of our cups. He made us laugh with his jokes. He played with our children. He left a good impression here and when he was candidate for state deputy he won. But the Chamber of Deputies didn't do one thing for the *favelados*. He doesn't visit us any more.

I classify São Paulo this way: The Governor's Palace is the living room. The mayor's office is the dining room and the city is the garden. And the favela is the back yard where they throw the garbage. . . .

At 8:30 that night I was in the favela breathing the smell of the filth mixed with the rotten earth. When I am in the city I have the impression that I am in a living room with crystal chandeliers, rugs of velvet, and satin cushions. And when I'm in the favela I have the impression that I'm a useless object, destined to be forever in a garbage dump. . . .

Yesterday I ate that macaroni from the garbage with fear of death, because in 1953

I sold scrap over there in Zinho. There was a pretty little black boy. He also went to sell scrap in Zinho. He was young and said that those who should look for paper were the old. One day I was collecting scrap when I stopped at Bom Jardim Avenue. Someone had thrown meat into the garbage, and he was picking out the pieces. He told me:

"Take some, Carolina. It's still fit to eat."

He gave me some, and so as not to hurt his feelings, I accepted. I tried to convince him not to eat that meat, or the hard bread gnawed by the rats. He told me no, because it was two days since he had eaten. He made a fire and roasted the meat. His hunger was so great that he couldn't wait for the meat to cook. He heated it and ate. So as not to remember that scene, I left thinking: I'm going to pretend I wasn't there. This can't be real in a rich country like mine. I was disgusted with that Social Service that had been created to readjust the maladjusted, but took no notice of we marginal people. I sold the scrap at Zinho and returned to São Paulo's back yard, the favela.

The next day I found that little black boy dead. His toes were spread apart. The space must have been eight inches between them. He had blown up as if made out of rubber. His toes looked like a fan. He had no documents. He was buried like any other "Joe." Nobody tried to find out his name. The marginal people don't have names. . . .

Oh, São Paulo! A queen that vainly shows her skyscrapers that are her crown of gold. All dressed up in velvet and silk but with cheap stockings underneath—the favela. . . .

What I think is interesting is when a person enters a bar or a saloon, very soon someone offers him a drink of *pinga* [liquor made from sugarcane]. Why don't they offer a kilo of rice, beans, candy, etc. . . ?

There are people here in the favela who

say that I'm trying to be a bigshot because I don't drink *pinga*. I am alone. I have three children. If I got the alcohol habit, my sons will not respect me. Even writing this I'm doing something stupid. I don't have to explain myself to anyone. To conclude: I don't drink because I don't like it, and that ends it. I prefer to put my money into books, rather than alcohol. If you think that I'm acting correctly, I beg you to say:

"Very well, Carolina!" . . .

December 31, 1959. João and Vera went to bed. I stayed up writing. Sleep came on me and I slept. I awoke with the whistle of the factory announcing the New Year. I thought of the São Silvestre races and of Manoel de Faria. I asked God to make him win the race. I also asked him to bless Brazil. [A footrace is traditionally run through the downtown streets of São Paulo on New Year's Eve, the feast of St. Sylvester. Carolina's favorite, Manoel de Faria, was nicknamed "The Racer."]

I hope that 1960 will be better than 1959. We suffered so much in 1959, that the people were singing:

"Go! Go for good!
I don't want you any more.
No, never more."

January 1, 1960. I got up at 5 and went to get water.

A São Paulo newspaperman discovered Carolina Maria de Jesus and her diaries. He published a portion of them, and the story created a sensation. Later all the notebooks were edited and published. Carolina Maria de Jesus, an exceptionally intelligent and talented person, became a celebrity. Her book sold in the thousands of copies. She moved from the favela into a better life. Still, she did not forget the past:

Today I had lunch in a wonderful restau-

rant and a photographer took my picture. I told him: "Write under the photo that Carolina who used to eat from trash cans now eats in restaurants. That she has come back into the human race and out of the Garbage Dump."

IN MEXICO CITY

In the city of Rio de Janeiro in 1960 there were two hundred favelas with a population of 337,500 persons. The favela population had nearly doubled over that of ten years before. Every Latin American city has its slums, where poverty and hunger are the central facts of life. For years the situation in Mexico City was no different from that in São Paulo:

Day after day, they sift through the mountains of garbage in the dumps outside Mexico City, occasionally stopping to stuff a torn sock, a battered book or a scrap of food into the voluminous [large] sacks slung over their shoulders. To Mexicans, these tattered figures are known as *pepenadores*—the scroungers. Poorer than the city's slum dwellers or the Indians of the countryside, 5,000 families live around— or *in*—the vile-smelling dumps. For years, officials simply ignored the problem. But now, 60 years after the Mexican Revolution promised to usher in an era of social justice, officials are finally making an effort to rescue the scroungers from the garbage heaps.

Most of them have known no other life than the dumps. Generations have been born and brought up there. They have also raised families and died in the houses of cardboard, wood and scrap metal they patched together in the midst of the malodorous squalor. The only money the scroungers earn comes from the 6,500 tons of rubbish thrown away daily by the 11 million people of greater Mexico City. The scavenged items are sold for a pittance [small amount] to self-appointed "dump bosses," who then resell them for a tidy profit. It is, by any standard, a degrading existence. "Many people who live here," one dump dweller [said], "eat things they find in the garbage."

Now, however, there is a glimmer of hope for the scroungers. The city has opened its first modern garbage-disposal-and-recycling plant and hired 60 scroungers to separate the garbage into categories such as paper, metal, plastic and bone in advance of the processing. It is still unpleasant work, but instead of the filthy clothing of the dumps, the workers wear bright orange uniforms and hard hats. They are paid $8 a day, far more than they ever received from the bosses, and they get social-security benefits and free medical treatment at the plant.

Over the next two years the city government plans to open a half-dozen more plants and provide jobs for more of the scroungers. Officials believe the plants will become self-supporting through the sale of the recycled material. But the realm of the white-coated scientists and gleaming equipment at the plant is a world away from the garbage dumps, and many of the scroungers actually prefer to stay where they are. Officials say that some who were allotted homes at bargain prices later sold them and moved back to their wretched shacks. "We may," says one official, "have to force them to move for their own good."

The city authorities believe there will always be a need for dumps for certain kinds of refuse, and the old, crippled and less ambitious among the scroungers are expected to remain behind among the heaps of garbage. "We may always have a problem with penenadores," says one official grimly. "But hopefully it will be nothing like the problem we have today."

The well-to-do of Latin America live somewhat differently. Here is a description of a recent party in Buenos Aires:

The guests began to arrive only around 11 last night at Mario's 10-room apartment in the Palermo district overlooking the city's most elegant causeway, the 10-lane Avenida Libertador. It was dawn before the last of the 26 revelers straggled out of the marble-lined lobby. . . .

Mario, the party's host, gave his guests a quick tour of the premises, pointing out the more recent art acquisitions. The Renaissance tapestry hanging in the sitting room had been bought by his grandparents, who made their fortune in ranching. But the 18th-century Spanish portraits were acquired only eight months ago.

The Spanish colonial-era ceramics, sitting atop the five-foot-high fireplace, were also recent purchases.

"I don't like them much myself, but Pedro assured me they were one of the best investments I could make at this point," Mario confided.

Pedro, one of the guests, works with a major art-auction house in Buenos Aires. In these hyperinflationary times, he explained, art has been one of the surest havens for the wealthy. . . .

It was almost 1 A.M. before the guests sat down for dinner under a glass chandelier imported from the Austrian-Hungarian Empire at the turn of the century. Six waiters, dressed in tuxedos and white gloves, served the four-course meal—fish mousse [a light spongy food], beef broth, filet mignon with embedded raisins and potato soufflé, and a cream meringue cake, along with red and white wines.

Mario graciously acknowledged the flow of compliments, . . . [moving to] the living room for coffee, cognac and dance music.

Unit 4
LATIN AMERICA IN THE TWENTIETH CENTURY

Throughout much of Latin American history, extreme rural poverty existed side by side with aristocratic landed wealth. There were, essentially, only two classes—lower and upper. Between these extremes there was a small middle class of self-employed people, such as shopkeepers and small businessmen; those working for salaries instead of hourly wages, such as teachers, managers, and technicians; and members of the professions, such as doctors and lawyers. The number in this class was so small that its impact on society was limited. But industrialization changed that. As economic opportunity increased, the middle class expanded. Today that group makes up from 40 to 50 percent of the population in such countries as Chile, Argentina, and Uruguay.

Industrialization has produced jobs and a higher standard of living for many people. This in turn has created a demand for goods that continues to outrun supply, bringing continual inflation to many Latin American countries.

In such nations as the United States and England the middle class proved a force for political compromise, stability, and democracy. But this has not been the case in Latin America. Extreme political positions, right-wing or left-wing, remain the rule, and uprisings and golpes de estado continue to be characteristic of the region. By and large, the Latin American middle class has not been willing to extend social, political, and economic benefits to those less well off. It has not supported the lowering or abolishing of property qualifications for voting, increased public expenditures on education and health and other social services, low-cost housing, or land reform. Recent political trends in Latin America have been toward a weakening of democratic institutions and toward military or dictatorial government. In such countries as Chile and Brazil, the middle class appears to have supported or at least accepted this trend.

On the other hand, the lower class has in some instances also supported military or dictatorial rule. This was the case in Argentina in the 1940s and early 1950s and in Cuba following revolution there in 1959.

Opposite: Highrises tower over ornate nineteenth century buildings in Montevideo, Uruguay.

Regardless of the form of government, there has been an increase in nationalistic feeling in Latin American countries. This has been expressed in efforts to expand industrially through the greater use of domestic capital instead of relying on foreign investment. Equally important, governments have shown a willingness to nationalize, or take over, such foreign-owned assets as oil wells and refineries.

Threats to foreign-owned property, as a consequence of either revolution or nationalization, have frequently brought Latin American nations into conflict with other countries, particularly the United States. Following the Latin American independence movement, the United States assumed political leadership in the Western Hemisphere and, especially in the twentieth century, invested billions of dollars in oil production, mining, and other enterprises. And from time to time the United States intervened in the affairs of Latin American nations, sometimes with armed force, for the stated purpose of protecting American business interests. Such inter-

Soccer fans fill Rio de Janeiro's Maracaña Stadium.

vention aroused resentment among Latin Americans and contributed to their feelings of nationalism.

Neither foreign nor domestic investment has been able to relieve the poverty in which millions of Latin Americans live. Nor has a trend toward right-wing governments. Rapid population growth easily outstrips the rate of economic development, and millions of poor are added each year to Latin America's population. Poverty and population growth are two of Latin America's urgent problems today and are likely to remain so. This is a fact that all Latin American governments, regardless of their political makeup, must face.

This final section dealing with Cuba, Chile, Argentina, and Brazil illustrates some Latin American problems and trends. It sketches the history of Latin American-United States relations and the development of Puerto Rico. The section concludes with some observations about current problems in Latin America.

Brazilian superstar Pélé played here before overflow crowds of 200,000 spectators.

Herding cattle on the plains of southern Brazil.

A PICTURE PORTFOLIO: LATIN AMERICA TODAY

Opposite: Banana pickers on a plantation in Honduras.

Manufacturing metal tanks in a plant in Bogotá, Colombia.

Samples of Brazilian coffee undergo an exacting taste test before the beans are graded.

Boatloads of fresh fruit and vegetables at a waterfront market in Pôrto Alegre, Brazil.

A farmers' market in Mexico.

Shopping at the Aurrera supermarket in Mexico City.

A class at the Universidad de los Andes, one of a dozen universities in Bogotá, Colombia.

Venezuelan sculptor Marisol transforms wood, paint, and found objects into a group called *The Party*.

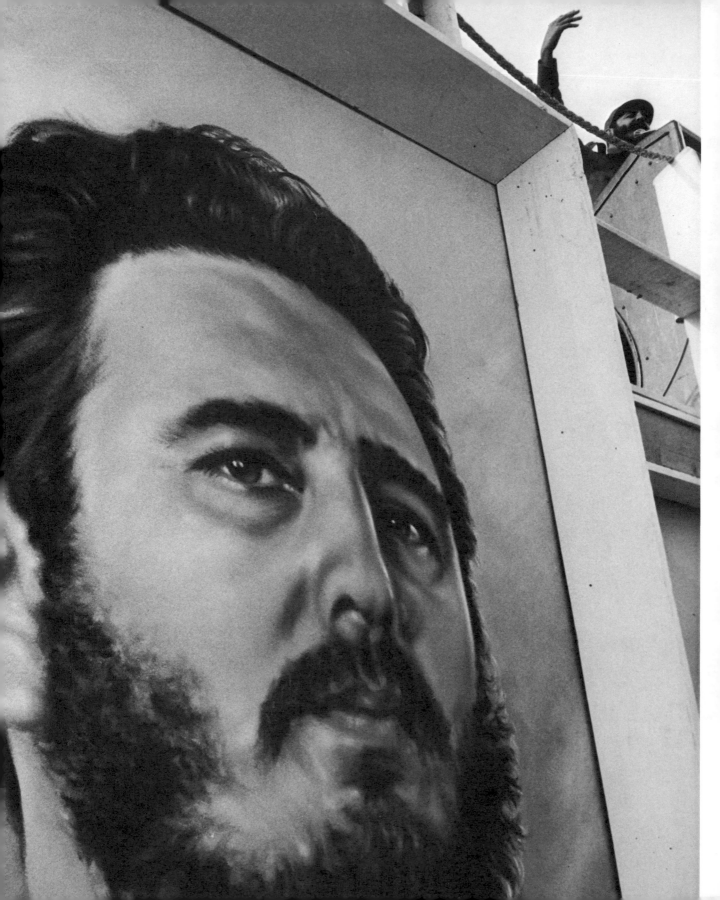

Although most of Spain's Latin American colonies won independence early in the 1800s, Cuba did not gain its freedom until the end of the nineteenth century.

Until the 1850s, there existed among Cubans little enthusiasm for independence. One reason for this was a stable colonial government backed by a strong army. Another was the relative prosperity criollo merchants and plantation owners enjoyed. Spain's trade policy for Cuba was somewhat more relaxed than it had been for other Latin American colonies. Cuban exports to countries other than Spain were taxed, but the export trade was not restricted to Spain. Cuban growers of coffee, tobacco, and especially sugar—which eventually made up 85 percent of the island's exports—could trade directly with other countries, and most years they profited. Another factor working against the development of an independence movement was the presence of a large black population, composed mainly of enslaved plantation hands. Many criollos feared that freedom from Spain might result in the establishment of a black-controlled nation, as in Haiti.

All this is not to say that interest in freeing Cuba from Spain was entirely absent. During the 1840s there were efforts to annex the island to the United States, led by Venezuelan-born Narciso López. Sought by Cuban police for his efforts on behalf of annexation, López fled to the United States in 1848. There he persuaded a number of prominent Americans that a majority of Cubans would welcome a United States takeover. Although many Americans opposed United States ownership of Cuba because of the presence of slavery there, President James Polk offered to buy the island from Spain. Spain declined to sell. López thereupon organized a force to invade Cuba. The United States government prevented this force from sailing. Undaunted, López formed another army of some six hundred men, landing with his troops in Cuba in 1850. Finding no popular support, the invaders quickly evacuated. López tried again in 1851, this time with about four hundred men. Again there was no Cuban support and on this occasion the Spanish captured López and executed him.

As had been the case in other Spanish colonies, Cuban political power and high government offices were reserved for the Spanish-born. This proved a source of increasing resentment among some criollos who wanted political power along with unrestricted Cuban trade. In 1868, led by plantation owner Carlos Manuel de Céspedes, a group of criollos demanded the establishment of a constitutional system of government for Cuba that would

Opposite: Dwarfed by a poster portrait, Fidel Castro addresses a 26th of July celebration in Santa Clara, Cuba. Castro speaks without notes, often eloquently, sometimes for hours.

provide for home rule, Cuban representation in the Spanish parliament, and freedom from trade restrictions. Following Spain's refusal to grant these demands, Céspedes organized an army that consisted of about 25,000 men, many of them freed slaves, to fight for Cuban independence. The conflict, which eventually cost the lives of 200,000 people and resulted in much property destruction, was confined mainly to guerrilla warfare in the mountainous eastern portion of Cuba. And it took the Spanish ten years to stamp out the last of the rebellion.

Another uprising began in 1895. This resulted in part from the economic depression of 1893 in the United States, which brought a severe drop in sugar prices, and in part from the activities of Cuban poet José Martí y Perez.

Residing at the time in New York City, Martí had long advocated Cuban independence in speeches and in published articles. Seeking to take advantage of economic unrest on the island, he returned there in 1895. Martí organized an army and, although possessing no military experience, took to the field to lead troops in person. He was killed in action six weeks after landing in Cuba. The rebellion continued under other leadership.

Americans in general sympathized with Cuban efforts to break free from Spain. This was partly due to their own attachment to independence and to democratic institutions and partly due to the propaganda of Martí and others. There was, however, no strong sentiment in favor of doing more than lending moral support to the rebels.

This changed, though, as American newspapers, particularly those in New York City, gave increasing attention to the conflict. They featured stories extremely sympathetic to the rebels and highly critical of Spanish efforts to put the rebellion down. Sensationalism sells newspapers, and such papers as the New York *Journal* and *World* were locked in a bat-

tle for readers to build up their advertising revenues. Both papers played up the horrible side of the measures Spain took to crush the rebellion, as circulation rose to more than one million copies a day. These stories particularly deplored the Spanish policy of reconcentration, which involved herding huge segments of the Cuban population into concentration camps in order to diminish active support of the rebel cause. Lack of adequate food and outbreaks of disease made them miserable places and brought death to thousands of people. On the other hand, the papers said little about rebel atrocities, which included killing persons who failed to support the rebel side and burning sugar plantations in an effort to drive the Spaniards from the island.

Thanks to newspaper emphasis on Spanish atrocities, both real and fancied, American public opinion swung to supporting the idea of United States intervention on the side of the rebels. Despite public opinion, however, few United States leaders wanted war with Spain. President William McKinley did not want war, and this feeling was shared by many American businessmen who had invested in Cuba's sugar plantations and mills and other enterprises. The Spanish government did not want war. And as the possibility of international conflict grew greater, Spain offered concessions to the Cuban rebels, including an end to the policy of reconcentration. Most important, Spain offered to grant Cubans self-government, but with final authority resting in a Spanish governor. Believing they would eventually win independence, rebel leaders refused the offer.

Early in 1898, President McKinley ordered the battleship *Maine* to Cuba to "protect American life and property" there. The *Maine* rode at anchor in Havana harbor. On February 15, 1898, a tremendous explosion sank the ship. Over 250 American lives were lost.

Americans blamed the Spanish for the deed. To this day, however, no one knows who or what caused the explosion. Even so, the incident was enough to push war fever to new heights. Yielding finally to public opinion, President McKinley asked Congress for a declaration of war against Spain. Congress complied. "Remember the *Maine!*" became the battlecry of the day.

In the sixteenth century, Spain had been the mightiest nation in the world. Now, at the end of the nineteenth century, it was at best a third-rate power. Within a few weeks the Spanish-American War was over. Spain was defeated and Cuba, independent. The United States received from Spain the Philippine Islands, Guam, and Puerto Rico. These islands became United States possessions.

DICTATORSHIP IN CUBA

Once their land was free of Spanish rule, Cuban leaders wrote a constitution to establish representative government. At the request of the United States, Cubans included in their constitution an amendment, part of which granted the United States the right to intervene in Cuba whenever necessary for the preservation of a stable, independent Cuban government. The amendment is known as the Platt Amendment, after the United States senator who suggested it. Cuba also granted the United States the right to build a naval base on Guantánamo Bay, in the eastern part of the island. The United States retains the base today.

United States medical teams working in Cuba after the war did much to improve sanitation and health on the island, eradicating yellow fever, which had long been a scourge there. As a consequence of United States money and efforts, transportation and communication facilities were improved. The United States became the most important market for Cuban sugar, the island's main crop. And by 1924, American businessmen had invested almost $1.5 billion in Cuba's sugar and tobacco plantations, electric light and telephone systems, banks, and hotels. In addition, mainly to protect these investments during times of revolution and civil turmoil, the United States intervened on several occasions. The United States occupied Cuba for three years from 1906 to 1909. And it did not give up its legal right to intervene until 1934.

The Cuban government itself was often notoriously corrupt. Those in power rewarded their friends and henchmen and punished their enemies. Little was done to bring education to the masses.

Members of a Cuban farm family.

In 1925 Cuba fell under the control of a full-fledged dictator, Gerardo Machado. He suppressed free speech and the press, jailed or executed opponents, and ruled with an iron hand. Machado was finally driven out in 1933.

At this point an army sergeant, Fulgencio Batista, became the power behind the government. Presidents were elected until 1940, when Batista assumed direct control for four years. Then he allowed the election of another president, as he did again in 1948. In 1952 Batista took over as dictator once again. The Batista government became more and more corrupt and, as has been the case with most caudillos, Batista enriched himself.

So did others in the Cuban government. Ramón Grau San Martín became president in 1944, Carlos Prío Socarrás in 1948. Most people believe that Grau stole the ceremonial emerald embedded in the Chamber of the Cuban Senate. A newsmagazine reported the departure of José Alemán, Minister of Education under Grau, when the Grau government left office:

> On the afternoon of October 10, 1948, he [Alemán] and some henchmen drove four Ministry of Education trucks into the Treasury building. All climbed out carrying suitcases. "What are you going to do, rob the Treasury?" joked a guard. "*Quién sabe?*" ["Who knows?"] replied baby-faced José Aleman. Forthwith his men scooped pesos, francs, escudos, lire, rubles, pounds sterling and about 19 million dollars in U.S. currency into the suitcases. The trucks made straight for the airfield, where a chartered DC-3 stood waiting.

Prío and his friends did as well, if not better, before they left office in 1952.

While some members of the middle class—including government officials—grew rather well-to-do, millions of Cubans remained poor.

Some skilled workers earned as much as 540 pesos a month—equal to 540 dollars. Many peasant families had to make do on about 7 pesos income per month.

When change came to Cuba, it occurred not because of overwhelming rebel force. It came because people were simply fed up with Batista, his dictatorships, his puppet presidents, and the brutality of his police. And the man who had the most to do with toppling Batista was a bearded young lawyer named Fidel Castro.

A REVOLUTIONARY LEADER

Born in 1927 the son of a wealthy landowner, Castro received a university education and earned a law degree. As a student he participated in an unsuccessful attempt to overthrow the dictator of the Dominican Republic, Rafael Leónidas Trujillo. That was in 1947. On July 26, 1953, Castro joined about two hundred young Cubans in an unsuccesful attack on the Moncada Barracks in Santiago de Cuba. Castro was among those captured and sentenced to prison. Batista pardoned him about eighteen months later.

A caudillo with remarkable popular appeal, Castro won support from Cuban workers, especially the unskilled. Students and other young people dissatisfied with the Cuban political situation also backed him, as did some white-collar and professional workers. Later he gained some peasant support.

Following his release from prison, Castro spent some time in Mexico. Then, early in 1956, he and about eighty followers "invaded" Cuba. Attacked by government forces, only a dozen members of the group reached safety in the Sierra Maestra, a rugged jungle region in eastern Cuba. One of the dozen was Fidel Castro.

In the mountains Castro organized and led

guerrilla forces. His group also seized land and livestock and distributed them to peasants. They established schools. By means of a powerful radio transmitter, the rebels fought Batista with words as well as deeds. Their repeated denunciations of the regime over Radio Rebelde did much to arouse people against the dictator.

The *Movimiento de 26 Julio*—the 26th of July Movement—ended in January 1959. Batista fled the country and the rebels entered Havana and Santiago de Cuba in triumph.

A SOCIALIST PROGRAM

The United States government recognized the new Cuban regime. Soon, however, as Castro's economic program for Cuba got underway, relations between the United States and Cuba cooled.

In June 1959 the Castro government decreed that individual landholding would be limited to a maximum of one thousand acres. Larger individual estates were seized by the government. Some of the land was distributed to peasants. Other land was made into large cooperative farms. The United States government protested the seizure of property in Cuba owned by Americans and demanded that it be paid for immediately. This the Castro government could not or would not do. In the meantime, thousands of Cubans who had lost their estates fled the island, most of them settling in the United States. They were later followed by thousands of professional and white-collar workers who did not wish to live under the Castro regime.

Castro took over more property held by United States companies in Cuba, refusing to pay for it, at least immediately. The United States government responded in July 1960 by first reducing its purchases of Cuban sugar. Castro then took over all American-owned sugar plantations and mills, along with oil refineries, telephone and electric companies, rail-

roads, hotels, and banks. In January 1961 the United States broke off diplomatic relations with Cuba.

A number of United States citizens, in government and out, concluded that Castro was a Communist. And they feared that, through the propaganda he aimed at various Latin American countries and the aid he furnished to left-wing revolutionaries, he would help spread communism in the Western Hemisphere.

All Latin American countries except Mexico followed the United States in ceasing to trade with Cuba. The Soviet Union became Cuba's main customer and supplier. Russia loaned the Castro government money and furnished it with arms. The Soviet Union also sent many technicians and advisors to Cuba to help further that country's industrial development.

With United States aid, Cuban refugees were armed and trained as an anti-Castro army, planning to invade Cuba and overthrow the Castro government. Much of the invading force was trained in Guatemala. No United States troops or pilots were to be involved in the invasion.

Castro became aware of the plans and when some fifteen hundred invaders moved ashore at the Bay of Pigs in Cuba in April 1961, his forces were waiting for them. In a brief battle Castro defeated the invaders, his troops taking some twelve hundred of them prisoner. Later, Castro demanded that the United States ransom the prisoners with fifty million dollars worth of food and medicine. The United States complied.

THE MISSILE CRISIS AND AFTER

The following year, in the fall of 1962, the United States government discovered that the Soviet Union was constructing nuclear missile launching sites in Cuba. Since Cuba lies but ninety miles off the coast of Florida, the United States government interpreted the presence of missiles on the island as a direct threat to its security.

The United States protested to the Soviet Union and demanded that the missile sites be removed. It threw a naval blockade around Cuba to prevent Soviet ships from reaching the island. During a few tense days in October 1962, nuclear war between the United States and the Soviet Union appeared a distinct possibility. Finally, the Soviet Union agreed to dismantle the sites. The missiles were removed from Cuba.

During the 1970s, Cuban-American relations thawed a little. However, in the 1980s under President Reagan, relations began to refreeze; the government again banned travel to Cuba and tightened trade restrictions. However, in 1987 in secret negotiations the United States agreed to accept Cuban immigrants if Cuba would take back Cubans being held in United States prisons. In 1989, under a United Nations-negotiated agreement, Cuba began to withdraw its troops stationed in Angola in southwest Africa. No one is sure of the direction Cuban-American relations will take under President George Bush; however, the Angolan withdrawal is likely to improve both Cuba's economy and its relations with the United States.

AN EVALUATION OF CASTRO'S CUBA

Observers who knew pre-Castro Cuba have reported extensive change as a consequence of the Castro regime. Food is rationed and housing is scarce. However, the cities are cleaner than before, free health care functions smoothly, free education offers equal opportunities and has boosted the literacy rate to 96 percent, and unemployment is nearly gone. Average monthly pay is $207; however, Cuba has begun to offer incentives whereby hardworking, educated specialists can earn a minimum of $576 monthly.

In 1989 Cuba celebrated the thirtieth anniversary of its revolution. Cubans are proud of improvements in education and medical care. Life expectancy exceeds that in most parts of Latin America. In recent years, Cuba has also improved its relationships with and increased its exports to other countries in Latin America.

Cuba continues to face problems, though. First, United States trade restrictions hamper Cuba's economy. Second, despite efforts to diversify the economy, sugar continues to make up 70 percent of the country's exports. When world sugar prices are low, the Cuban economy suffers. Third, Cuba continues to rely heavily on Soviet economic aid, having accepted $4.5 billion a year from the Soviets in the late 1980s. Fourth, Castro allowed almost no freedom of speech or of the press. Unlike the Soviet leaders in the late 1980s, Castro refuses to liberalize rules on dissent. Here are one visitor's comments on a trip to Cuba:

There are some obvious reasons for Cuba's economic troubles. The U.S. trade embargo has hurt, for most Cuban machinery, including that of the sugar mills, came from America before the revolution. Cuba has been unable to obtain adequate spare parts. Another dislocation was caused by the exodus of the middle class. Since the revolution, 452,000 Cuban refugees—most of them managers, shopkeepers, professionals —have fled to the United States. That is an enormous number of skilled people from a country that had a population of only six million in 1959 and has a population of nine million now. Their departure, of course, has eased the transformation of Cuba from a bourgeois [middle-class] society dependent on American capitalism to that of a Communist society held up by the Soviet Union. But it was a great price to pay.

Many American analysts put even more blame on the romantic attempts by Fidel Castro to manage a complex economy through personal charisma [magnetic charm or appeal], rhetoric, and energy. The sugar fiasco of 1970 is the main evidence. In that year, Castro put his prestige behind a campaign to cut ten million tons of sugarcane. He rushed across the countryside urging all Cubans to join the harvest. It was as if he were back in the old days, leading an attack against Batista's forces.

Although Cuba did produce more sugar that year than ever before or since, the harvest was 1.5 million tons short of its goal. Perhaps more important, the economy was disrupted because of the numbers of Cubans who left their regular work to cut cane. Milk and steel production dropped heavily. Fidel himself proclaimed that his campaign was a failure. . . .

There appears now to be a growing institutionalization of the Cuban government. Instead of Fidel rushing about like an emperor making decisions on the spot, analysts believe, decisions are now made by technicians and planners, advised by Russian experts. Perhaps this accounts for the steady though slow recovery of the economy since the most depressed days of a few years ago.

Cuban students drill before a billboard that celebrates one of Castro's victories.

Beginning in 1932, when a new constitution took effect, Chile enjoyed a reputation as a democratic, stable country. Governments came and went without much turmoil. Like so many Latin American countries, however, Chile had a latifundia problem. In the late 1960s, about 5 percent of the population owned 70 percent of the land. Also, Chile's economy was based mainly on a single product, copper, whose price on the world market went up and down. This made income uncertain from year to year. Many Chileans, especially tenant farmers and unskilled city dwellers, lived in poverty, earning as little as fifty cents a day.

Eduardo Frei Montalva, a distinguished and scholarly leader of the Christian Democratic party, became president of Chile in 1964. Frei promised improvements in the lives of Chileans. Said he upon election:

> My administration intends that in an ever-increasing manner the peasants will be owners of the land and that property will not be concentrated in the hands of the few; that those who work in the fields will have a just wage and income, and that the laws of the nation will be strictly obeyed. Its aim is that all Chilean families will live in their own homes in a decent community where their children can live in dignity and happiness. It intends to promote economic development and free initiative so that we may increase the production of foodstuffs, expand our industries, and develop our mineral resources for the benefit of Chile.
>
> It proposes to stop inflation, to protect the value of the currency, to provide steady employment and give youth an opportunity; to break the rigidity of a social order that no longer responds to the demands of the time, and thereby afford access to a real participation in the wealth and the advantages which mark contemporary societies.

Subsidiaries of Kennecott and Anaconda, two United States corporations, were the largest copper companies operating in Chile. The Frei government persuaded them to agree that 50 percent of the profits they earned would remain in Chile. At the same time, the Chilean government acquired a majority interest in Kennecott's El Teniente mine, producer of 40 percent of Chile's copper. This afforded American owners a tax benefit and appeared to be a bulwark against future government confiscation. About ten million acres of land were distributed to landless peasants. But the Chilean

Opposite: A busy street in Santiago, Chile's capital and largest city.

upper class, composed of large landowners and big businessmen, was not interested in helping Frei fulfill his election promises.

Considerable change occurred, however, during the next administration. It began with the selection of Salvador Allende Gossens as president in October 1970.

Allende came from a well-to-do family of Valparaíso, Chile's leading port. After earning a medical degree at the University of Chile, he practiced medicine for five years in provincial cities. But Allende's main interest was politics, his principal ambition to be president.

For several years Allende served in the Chamber of Deputies and the Senate. Three times he ran for president. Three times he lost. Then, in the September 1970 elections, Allende won a slightly larger percentage of votes than his two opponents. None had a majority. Consequently, following the Chilean constitution, the Congress was to choose between the two candidates having the most votes. As was traditional, Congress endorsed the leading candidate, Allende.

ALLENDE COMES TO POWER

Considering the philosophy Allende took into office with him, it may seem remarkable that he won the presidency. Allende had been the candidate of a coalition called *Unidad Popular,* or Popular Unity. This was composed of Socialists, Communists, most of the Radical party, and some Christian Democrats. Allende himself was a Marxist, a person who believed in the eventual abolition of private property and in the even distribution of wealth. To most people, this means a Communist dictatorship. Allende, however, was no dictator. He had won office by constitutional means, the first Marxist ever to become head of a government through free and open elections. There was no reason to believe

that he would destroy such democratic freedoms as free speech and press. Still, if Allende were to carry out a Marxist program, it would mean government takeover of industries as well as land.

Following Allende's selection, rumors and stories flew about what might happen. Wrote the North American journalist Joseph Kraft:

Almost everybody at the Golf Club had a personal grievance to air. A lawyer said that the foreign firms he represents are beginning to close down operations. The wife of a broker, who has her luggage packed, ready for a getaway, said her husband went to the Bolsa [stock exchange] every day but had nothing to do, because trading there had almost stopped since the election. A young industrial designer reported that all his orders were cancelled after the vote. A visiting member from the Polo Club complained that two polo fields had been set aside for housing projects. But despite these intimations of a deluge to come, hardly anybody was getting out. Indeed, some who left Chile just after the election, on September 4th [1970] had come back. "I suppose that it's too good to last," the wife of the lawyer said. "My sister in New York calls us every day on the phone. She says terrible things will happen and that we must come out. But we're not leaving yet. After all, where else can we live as well as in Chile?"

The same reporter also talked with a Communist senator:

When I asked him whether he thought Chile would become the second Cuba in the hemisphere, he said, "The Cuban and Chilean experiences are very different. Cubans achieved independence from Spain at the end of the nineteenth century. We achieved it at the beginning. They had a military dictatorship for years. We have a century and a half of almost uninterrupted parliamentary government. Most of us in the Communist Party have worked in the parliamentary system for thirty years." I asked him about Chile's relations with other Latin American countries—particularly Argentina and Brazil, which had expressed misgivings about the Allende regime. He said, "We are not exporters of revolution. We do not imagine ourselves as the liberators of Argentina or Brazil or any other country. We hope for good relations with the United States. We even hope some of the Chileans who have fled there will come back."

Salvador Allende himself appeared confident.

Dr. Allende seemed far shorter in person than I had expected, possibly because pictures reflect the lift given by an upward tilt of the head and a wave in his hair. The President is all motion when he talks, with features doing a kind of dance, hands sawing the air. He has a nervous habit of knocking his knees together. At the outset, he aired some views on how much the dangers of a Communist takeover had been exaggerated in the United States. "We don't hide what we do," he said. "You can go outside and see for yourself. No liberties have been sus-

The rich El Teniente copper mine lies ten thousand feet up in the Andes in the crater of an extinct volcano.

pended. There is no censorship of the press. Everybody said when I came in there would be no more elections. But now all the parties are preparing for the municipal elections in April. And if we had national elections today, more than 50 percent would vote for the government."

COLLAPSE OF CHILE'S ECONOMY

At the time Allende took office, the Chilean economy was in poor shape. Inflation was running at a rate of about 35 percent a year. Industries were operating below 50 percent of capacity. Only about a million of Chile's nine million citizens could be described as economically secure, with sufficient income to live decently.

The Allende administration began by nationalizing copper mines, banks, and insurance companies. These actions did not improve the economy, however. Copper production fell off as foreign technicians fled the country. A sharp decline in the price of copper did not help matters either.

Along with a drop in copper production went a decrease in agricultural production. The Allende government granted many peasants small farms of five to twenty acres. While peasants welcomed the opportunity to own land, their production did not prove to be as great and as efficient as that of large farms. Drought as well as low agricultural prices also curtailed farm production. The need to compensate owners for their land left the Allende government with insufficient funds to pay for imported food.

Inflation proved to be Allende's most difficult problem. Prices during 1972 alone increased about a hundred percent. Chileans protested. On one occasion, women marched through the streets of Santiago beating on pans to demonstrate against high prices. Shortly after assuming power, the Allende government raised wages 35 percent. Later, wages were increased further. But they did not keep pace with inflation.

In 1972 the Allende government decided to take over the trucking industry, the chief means of transporting goods in Chile. This caused a nationwide strike. For many days, scarcely anything moved. Allende finally backed down.

Since Unidad Popular held a minority of seats in the Congress, Allende experienced opposition in getting his programs adopted. Communists and Socialists complained that he did not move quickly enough to make Chile a truly Marxist nation. Conservatives, on the other hand, criticized him for moving in that direction at all. In response to opposition, Allende withdrew the advertising of government and state-owned industry from newspapers that criticized him. He also closed down some opposition radio stations.

THE ARMY SEIZES POWER

On September 1973, when his term of office still had three years to run, the army—which had previously supported Allende—staged a coup. Forces led by Augusto Pinochet Ugarte seized control of the government. For days Chile was wracked by civil war. Thousands of persons died. Allende himself died in the presidential palace in Santiago. Whether he was murdered or committed suicide remains a question. The army clamped a tight lid on Chile. Reports said that thousands of people suspected of opposing the new regime—some said three thousand, others said fifteen thousand—were rounded up and jailed. Many were shot outright. Others, according to reports, were tortured before being given brief trials and led to execution.

Following the coup, disclosures were made

that seemed to indicate that, prior to Allende's selection as president, the United States had given active support to Allende's opponents. Working through the Central Intelligence Agency, or CIA, the United States government was said to have given several million dollars to Allende's opponents.

The CIA had been established after World War II to coordinate information from other countries that might be useful in maintaining the security of the United States. Evidence seemed to indicate that members of the CIA had exceeded their legal authority by attempting to influence political events in some Latin American nations.

United States funds had reportedly gone to labor unions to finance strikes and to politicians and newspapers that opposed Allende. There were reports that International Telephone and Telegraph, a United States corporation that owned utility systems in Chile, also supplied money to try to keep Allende out of office. Some saw these actions as part of the United States policy of trying to prevent the spread of communism in the Western Hemisphere. On the other hand, the Soviet Union and Cuba supplied Allende with funds.

The Pinochet regime returned property to foreign companies, and some of them increased their investments in Chile. At the same time, the Pinochet government abolished freedom of speech, press, and assembly. It outlawed political parties, dissolved the Congress, and tortured political opponents.

In 1980, voters approved a constitution that set Pinochet's term of office to end in March 1990. In the fall of 1988, Pinochet held a plebiscite asking voters to extend his term to 1997. Despite fifteen years of repression, Pinochet's opponents organized a strong campaign and 55 percent of the voters rejected extending Pinochet's term. Chile is scheduled to have a new presidential election in December 1989.

Marxist supporters of Chile's Salvador Allende. The painted slogan at left translates: "Don't play games with the people."

ARGENTINA
Chapter 14

Cuba and Chile were not the only Latin American nations to undergo change in an attempt to solve their political and economic problems. In Argentina, beginning in the 1940s, urban workers became a powerful force in changing governments.

LANDED WEALTH IN ARGENTINA

Latifundism—land ownership by the few—had been the most important factor in Argentina's economy since colonial days.

Bernardino Rivadavia, president of the Argentine confederation in 1826–27, tried to promote the settlement of the grasslands by leasing public lands to colonists. After his overthrow, however, title to these public lands went to a handful of cattlemen. By 1830, some 21 million acres of land in the public domain had gone to five hundred private owners. Under Juan Manuel de Rosas, governor of Buenos Aires who became the virtual dictator of Argentina between 1835 and 1852, public lands were further depleted. He waged wars against the Indians, and then divided their lands among his supporters. In 1879–80, Indian campaigns led by General Julio A. Roca cleared the Indians from much of southern Argentina.

Another 150 million acres of Indian land found their way into the hands of a few.

During the second half of the nineteenth century, more than two million immigrants streamed into Argentina, doubling that nation's population. Most of them came from Italy and Spain. Unable to buy land for the most part, some worked as hired hands or as tenants on estancias, large estates or cattle ranches. The rest settled in the cities where they found work as shopkeepers, waiters, taxi drivers, and laborers in meat-packing and other new industries.

Argentina had its local and national caudillos. It experienced periods of dictatorial rule, as under Rosas. There were a few periods during which strictly constitutional governments operated, as under the educator and newspaperman Domingo Faustino Sarmiento, who was president from 1865 to 1874. But no government existed without the support of the large landowners who, along with a growing number of industrialists, dominated Argentina's economic, social, and political life.

Opposite: Juan Perón and his wife Eva leave the presidential palace on their way to the Teatro Colón on Argentina's independence day, 1950.

THE RISE OF JUAN PERÓN

This was true, at least, until the 1940s. Then, one of Argentina's more remarkable men, Juan Domingo Perón, became aware of the political strength of the growing working class. Perón managed to win over the urban workers, who supported him with their votes or, surging through city streets, with their muscle.

Born of lower-middle-class parents in 1895, Perón moved with his family at age ten from their small village to Buenos Aires. There he completed his schooling and entered the national military academy. He moved steadily upward in the military ranks and in 1939 served as military attaché at the Argentine embassy in Rome. Italy was then ruled by the dictator Benito Mussolini, whom Perón greatly admired. He also admired Adolf Hitler, who was dictator of Germany. Perón became convinced that dictatorship would be the chief form of government in the world.

Shortly after returning to Argentina, Perón married the actress Eva Duarte. Argentines later would know her fondly as Evita.

In 1943 Perón joined other army officers to stage a golpe de estado, after which the army took over the government. Perón himself served as secretary of labor, minister of war, and vice-president. He used the labor post in particular to build up strong support among workers and the urban poor. This group came to be referred to as the descamisados, "the shirtless ones." Gathering political strength, Perón gradually assumed dictatorial power.

Perón controlled the army and the labor unions. He won support from the Catholic church by allowing religious instruction in public schools. He kept schools and universities under his thumb by dismissing thousands of teachers and professors and replacing them with loyal followers. He closely controlled the Argentine press and radio networks and in 1951 closed down the country's largest and most influential paper, La Prensa. Although Perón seldom had his opponents shot, he did fill the jails with thousands of them.

A commanding speaker, Perón could sway crowds easily. Evita was almost always at his side. Nursing bitter memories of a lower-class upbringing, Evita harangued listeners about the evil ways of the Argentine wealthy. She spent much of her time in charitable work, mingling with the people. The descamisados idolized both Peróns, especially Evita.

In 1946, promising to mold Argentina into a world power, Perón won election as president. He spent a good deal of public money on charity, hospitals, and other social services to aid workers and the poor. He spent to increase Argentina's military might. And he bought out foreign-owned railroad and utility companies. These huge expenditures helped drain the public treasury and led to tax increases. The Perón government rigidly controlled farm prices, which benefited city dwellers. Hampered by price controls, Argentine farmers became discouraged and farm production fell off. Living costs rose. Argentina had been among the world's leading exporters of beef and mutton. It had produced a great deal of wheat. Now the nation had to import food and Argentineans experienced "meatless days."

THE PERÓN REGIME IN TROUBLE

The army, which had supported Perón's rise to power, became more and more dissatisfied with what it viewed as Perón's favoritism toward the working class. The army also objected to Perón's plan, offered in August 1951, to run Evita as candidate for the vice-presidency. If she won election, in the event of Perón's death she would become president and commander-in-chief of the armed forces. This was too much for the generals, and Perón had to back down.

The beautiful and popular Evita died of cancer in 1952, aged thirty-three. After that, Perón's fortunes moved steadily downhill.

A Perón plan to organize youth into semi-military squadrons to promote his glorification and to teach in schools that Peronism was the "one true faith" of all Argentineans landed Perón in trouble with the Catholic church. He fell further from grace when he proposed legislation to separate church and state. Continued high taxes displeased the wealthy. Opposition mounted as the failure of Perón's economic policies became obvious.

Navy pilots attempted a golpe de estado in June 1955. The effort failed. In response, Peronist mobs took to the streets in Buenos Aires, burning and looting. Three months later, a better organized rebellion toppled Perón. But the army continued to rule the country.

Perón found refuge first in Paraguay, then in other Latin American countries. Finally, in 1960, he left Latin America to live in Spain. There he married his secretary, a former dancer, María Estela Martínez, who preferred the name Isabel.

This was not the end of Perón as far as Argentina was concerned, however. Following Perón's ouster, Argentina was governed by a succession of eight chief executives, only two of them elected. Attempts at civilian government ended with military takeover. The country also suffered from constant inflation.

Perón continued to enjoy support in Argentina, particularly among the working class, which commanded a third of the vote. Finally, in November 1972, Perón returned to Argentina, continued on a whirlwind tour of several Latin American countries, and went back to Spain. His supporters then chose Hector J. Campora as a presidential candidate with the understanding that if Campora won he would quit in Perón's favor. Campora won the election in March 1973 and within a few months he resigned. New elections were held in September 1973, with Perón running for president and his wife Isabel for vice-president. They took 62 percent of the vote.

Perón's return to power at age seventy-eight was troublesome and short-lived. He surrounded himself with conservative advisors and no longer cultivated labor union support. Argentina's economic situation did not improve.

On July 1, 1974, Perón died. His widow became president, the first woman to hold such an office in Latin America. Isabel Perón's regime was plagued by continued inflation and political turmoil. Terrorism became common.

On March 23, 1976, a military junta, or council, ousted President Isabel Perón. The junta suspended all political parties, arrested leftists and Peronists, and carried on a campaign of terrorism and torture against suspected opponents. Inflation, a climbing foreign debt, and a domestic austerity program eroded support for the junta, however. In 1982, President Galtieri, the commander of the army, launched an invasion of the Falkland Islands, also known as the Malvinas, under British control but claimed by the Argentines. Britain's swift defeat of the Argentine forces led to the fall of the military junta and a return to civilian government under President Raúl Alfonsín at the end of 1983.

The Alfonsín government has faced two major problems. One is how to treat the military rulers responsible for torturing and killing people. Only a few have been brought to justice. Galtieri was sentenced to twelve years in prison, primarily for his negligence during the Falklands War. Attempts to indict other leaders, though, have caused several minor rebellions in the military.

The other issue is how to promote economic growth and reduce the $55 billion foreign debt. In 1988, Alfonsín announced one novel plan to encourage economic growth in southern Argentina. He said that by 1990 Argentina would move its capital from Buenos Aires to Viedma, a small coastal city farther south.

The first emperor of Brazil, Dom Pedro I, assumed the throne in 1822, at age twenty-four. He experienced a stormy reign.

A convention met in 1823 to write a constitution for the newly independent nation. Bitter quarreling between native-born and Portuguese-born delegates led Dom Pedro to dismiss the convention. He issued his own constitution the following year. The document guaranteed protection of civil rights and provided for a legislature. But it also granted the monarch power to dissolve the legislature whenever he wished and to appoint governors and select senators for the legislature. Dom Pedro's action brought about a rebellion in Brazil's four northern provinces, a rebellion that the army quickly suppressed.

Without consulting the national assembly, Dom Pedro reached an agreement with Portugal to obtain recognition of Brazil's independence. In return the emperor agreed to pay Portugal two million English pounds as compensation for the loss of its colony.

Then an uprising in a southern province which is now Uruguay was supported by Argentina. The rebellion led to war between Argentina and Brazil, which ended with Uruguay's independence. The loss of Uruguay added further to Dom Pedro's unpopularity.

When King John of Portugal died in 1826, Dom Pedro spent huge sums of money in an attempt to gain the Portuguese throne for his eldest daughter, Maria de Glória. The national assembly criticized Dom Pedro's Portuguese policies and refused to grant him all the money he requested to maintain his court. In 1829 the emperor dissolved the assembly to rule alone.

By 1830 Dom Pedro had lost all the popular support he had enjoyed at the beginning of his reign, as well as that of the landowners. Banding together early in 1831, plantation owners and other political leaders won support from the army and forced the emperor to abdicate in favor of his five-year-old son.

Dom Pedro II assumed actual power in 1840 when he was almost fifteen. And he proved an able and popular ruler. During his reign, Brazil prospered economically, particularly with respect to coffee and sugar sales.

Dom Pedro II was not without opposition, however. He tolerated Protestants and Freemasons, which displeased Catholic church officials. Slavery was abolished in Brazil in 1888, which diminished the emperor's support among planters. Intellectuals came to believe that monarchy was old-fashioned and had no place in the New World. Army and navy officers became increasingly dissatisfied because Dom Pedro discouraged their participation in

Opposite: The Foreign Ministry at Brasília framing a reflecting pool. Brazilians have nicknamed the twin buildings in the background "the wind sandwich."

politics and did not grant them honors or pay raises.

Late in 1889, army leaders removed the sixty-four-year-old Pedro II and placed him on a ship for Portugal. Later he settled in France, where he died in 1891. That same year, Brazil got a new constitution that established a representative government without a monarch.

DICTATORS AND PRESIDENTS

Following the departure of Dom Pedro II, Brazil's political experience was much the same as that of other Latin American nations. There were constitutionally elected governments and occasional dictatorships. Most of the time local caudillos ruled in the provinces.

Washington Luiz Pereira de Souza, former governor of the coffee province of São Paulo, served as president of Brazil from 1926 to 1930. That year, according to custom, the presidency should have gone to a politician from Minas Gerais province. Instead, Washington Luiz and other political leaders gave their support to Julio Prestes, also of São Paulo. The angry politicians of Minas Gerais responded by putting up Getulio Vargas, former governor of the cattle province of Rio Grande do Sul. Prestes won a bitterly contested election. The resulting rebellion ended in October 1930 with Vargas installed in the presidential palace. And Vargas was to prove a durable executive, ruling during most of the years between 1930 and 1954.

The Vargas regime did much to expand and industrialize the Brazilian economy. It promoted the manufacturing of textiles, chemicals, leather and rubber products, and cement, protecting new industries with high tariffs. By 1938 the total value of Brazil's industrial output was three times that of agriculture and livestock. Among the industrial achievements of the Vargas administration was the establishment of a huge iron and steel plant at Volta Redonda, in São Paulo province. Vargas also tried to improve the condition of the workers. He abolished child labor and set standards regarding wages and hours and equal pay for women.

At the end of his first term as president, in 1937, Vargas dispensed with elections and made himself dictator. He was deposed in 1945, but then won election as a senator representing Rio Grande do Sul. In 1950 he was once again elected president.

Now seventy-three years old, Vargas did not attempt to rule as dictator as he had in the past. But his refusal to welcome more foreign capital to continue Brazil's economic expansion drew criticism from business interests. A drop in coffee prices stirred further criticism of his economic policies. The army became increasingly hostile. Finally, when it appeared that the army intended to depose him, Vargas committed suicide in August 1954.

Elections held in 1956 placed Juscelino Kubitschek in the presidency. His administration concentrated on economic expansion and promoting Brazilian nationalism. Some eleven thousand miles of new roads and highways were completed, the merchant fleet was expanded into Latin America's largest, and steel production doubled. Oil production also increased, and several new hydroelectric plants were built.

During the Kubitschek administration Brazil's government moved from Rio de Janeiro to Brasília, a new capital city created in the north central portion of the country, about six hundred miles from the coast. Building a new capital in the wilderness recognized the growing economic and political importance of Brazil's vast interior. The act was also a symbol of nationalism, indicating the Brazilian people's determination to develop their natural resources on their own insofar as possible.

Brazilian architect Oscar Niemeyer designed monumental structures to house Brazil's governmental bodies. Developing new and radical methods of working with reinforced concrete, he created buildings that looked like gigantic shells, sails, and arching bowls. Brasília was dedicated in April 1960. Unfortunately, its construction cost of about $700 million nearly depleted the national treasury.

Kubitschek left office in January 1961 following the election of Jânio Quadros as president. Quadros tried to control inflation by halting wage increases and cutting government spending. Then, seven months after his inauguration, he resigned and began a voyage around the world. The reasons behind his resignation have never been satisfactorily explained.

At the time, Vice-President João Goulart was just returning from a visit to China. The Brazilian ministry considered him pro-Communist, and before he was allowed to assume the presidency, the army forced a change in the constitution, replacing the presidential system with a parliamentary system. A cabinet headed by a prime minister would be responsible to the legislature, which the army controlled. In 1963 Goulart arranged for a plebiscite—a yes or no vote—on the question of returning to the presidential system of government. Brazilian voters approved the change in the constitution that restored the presidential system, but Goulart did not remain long as president. His efforts at land reform aroused opposition from wealthy landowners. His inability to check inflation, along with his pro-labor sympathies, displeased the middle class. Food shortages hit hard at the poor. There were numerous strikes, some marked by violence. In the eyes of many Brazilians, Goulart seemed much too tolerant of the Brazilian Communist party. This was particularly true of the military, and the army deposed Goulart in March 1964. Following the coup, although elections were held regularly, the army remained in control of Brazil's government into the 1980s.

In 1979, General João Baptista de Oliveira Figueirdo took office as president. He vowed to return Brazil to civilian-led democracy. In 1985, Tancredo Neves became Brazil's first civilian president since 1964. Neves died a few months later, but his vice president, José Sarney, succeeded him without difficulty.

Economic problems continued to plague Brazil during the 1980s. By 1987, Brazil's foreign debt was $111 billion. High inflation and unemployment have made debt repayment difficult. Despite Brazil's tremendous natural resources, millions of people live in poverty.

Brazil's economic problems, however, have not undercut its return to democracy. In October 1988, Brazil adopted a new constitution, that guaranteed the basic rights of all citizens and established democratic procedures. This marked the end of two decades of military rule and transition to civilian government. The constitution called for a presidential election in 1989 to choose a successor to President Sarney. The voting age was lowered to sixteen.

The constitution established limits on the power of government in order to prevent the abuses that had occurred under military rule. For example, the president can no longer make new laws by presidental decree. All forms of government censorship have been abolished, and the use of torture was specifically outlawed. All major economic policy decisions must now be approved by the legislature.

The new constitution also helps working people by cutting the work week from forty-eight to forty-four hours. Maternity and paternity leave are now guaranteed, as is the workers' right to form unions and to strike.

The constitution also calls for a nationwide vote in 1993 to decide the type of government. Brazilians will be able to select a presidential, parliamentary, or monarchical form of government.

RELATIONS WITH THE UNITED STATES

Chapter 16

The United States has been a factor of tremendous influence in Latin American countries. The American Revolution helped inspire revolutions in Latin America which led to independence. United States trade and investment have been enormously important. And so have attitudes and policies the United States government has displayed.

Black revolt in Haiti toward the end of the eighteenth century quickly drew the attention of United States citizens. Because slavery existed in the United States at the time, many feared the Haitian example would touch off slave rebellions at home. There *were* slave uprisings, but none appear to have been influenced by events in Haiti.

Generally, however, people in the United States applauded Latin American efforts to gain independence. And by the 1820s, Americans were coming to look upon the entire Western Hemisphere as an area of special interest to the United States.

Rumors had spread that Austria, France, Prussia, and Russia planned to help Spain recover its Latin American territories. In addition, Russia had made a colony of Alaska and there were indications that it might colonize south of there.

Great Britain, like the United States, wanted Latin American nations to retain their independence. When Spain and Portugal ruled the region, Britain's trade there had been limited. Independence brought freedom to trade. To see that trade remained free, Britain asked the United States to join in a declaration warning other European governments against attempting to assert authority in Latin America.

The United States was not a powerful nation. Great Britain, possessing the world's strongest fleet, was. Secretary of State John Quincy Adams concluded that Britain would use its fleet to protect its trade whether that country was party to a joint declaration or not. Adams consequently argued that issuing a solitary declaration would increase the prestige of the United States. "It would be more candid," he said, "as well as more dignified, to avow our principles explicitly to Russia and France, than to come in as a cock-boat in the wake of the British man-of-war."

President James Monroe accepted Adams's advice and in his annual message to Congress on December 2, 1823, he included two statements which became known as the Monroe Doctrine. Referring to the Russian presence on the Pacific coast, he said:

In the discussions . . . the occasion has been judged proper for asserting . . . that the

Opposite: Eighty-six Venezuelan farmers become new landowners through the Alliance for Progress. A ceremony attended by John F. Kennedy in 1961.

American continents, by the free and independent condition which they have assumed and maintained, are henceforth not to be considered as subject for future colonization by any European power.

Later in his address, regarding European intervention in Latin America, Monroe said:

The political system of the allied [European] powers is essentially different . . . from that of America. . . . We owe it, therefore, to candor [honesty] and to the amicable [friendly] relations existing between the United States and those powers to declare that we should consider any attempt on their part to extend their system to any portion of this hemisphere as dangerous to our peace and safety.

With the existing colonies or dependencies of any European power we have not interfered and shall not interfere. But with the Governments who have declared their independence . . . we could not view any interposition [interference] for the purpose of oppressing them, or controlling in any other manner their destiny, by any European power in any other light than as the manifestation [display] of an unfriendly disposition toward the United States.

APPLYING THE MONROE DOCTRINE

There was no need for the United States to try to enforce the Monroe Doctrine in any way when Spain attempted to regain Mexico in 1829. A Mexican army under Santa Anna easily defeated the invaders. When France invaded Mexico in 1862 and made Maximilian emperor there, the United States, though in the midst of civil war, protested and continued to recognize Benito Juárez as Mexico's president. Once the Civil War ended, the United States again urged France to withdraw from Mexico, stating that the American people "are disposed to regard with impatience the continued intervention of France." In 1867 Russia pulled out of the Western Hemisphere, selling Alaska to the United States. The Monroe Doctrine came into play in the 1890s during a boundary dispute between Venezuela and the colony of British Guiana. The dispute was finally settled without war.

Speaking of the boundary dispute and the Monroe Doctrine in 1895, Secretary of State Richard Olney declared: "Today the United States is practically sovereign on this continent, and its fiat [command] is law upon the subjects to which it confines its interposition." Olney's words signaled the beginning of an era of United States intervention that would arouse deep resentment among many Latin Americans.

The United States intervened in Cuba in 1898 and helped Cubans win independence from Spain. Congress then passed the Platt Amendment which was added to the Cuban constitution. The amendment contained several provisions:

First, Cuba was not to allow any foreign power to secure even partial control of the island.

Second, Cuba would not go deeply into debt.

Third, the United States could intervene in Cuba to preserve order and maintain the island's independence.

And, finally, Cuba would sell or lease to the United States sites for coaling and naval stations.

Cuba experienced a revolution in 1906 and the United States intervened. Troops remained on the island until 1909. The United States intervened once again in 1917. The Platt Amendment was repealed in 1934.

BUILDING A CANAL IN PANAMA

Early in the twentieth century, the United States wished to build a canal across Panama. A canal would assist in defense because warships could be transferred more quickly between the Atlantic and the Pacific than if they had to sail around the southern tip of South America. A canal would also aid international trade. A French company had tried to construct a waterway across Panama but had failed. The United States government looked favorably on taking over French interests there and was willing to pay forty million dollars for these interests.

Panama was then a province of Colombia. Although the Colombian government seemed agreeable to parting with land for the canal, it held out for a larger sum than the ten million dollars the United States offered for it. If the French company did not sell its rights before they expired in October 1904, the rights and properties would revert to Colombia, which had granted the concession to build a canal to the Frenchmen. In that case, the Colombian government hoped to receive the forty million dollars the United States was willing to pay.

A Panamanian rebellion against Colombia,

United States officials, some bringing their wives and children, on an inspection tour of the locks during construction of the Panama Canal.

probably helped by agents of Frenchmen eager to sell their rights to a canal, began in 1903. As the uprising got underway, the United States stationed a warship off Panama to prevent Colombia from transporting troops there. The rebellion succeeded. Panama became an independent nation. United States President Theodore Roosevelt was said to have boasted: "I took Panama." Work on the canal commenced in 1904 and it was opened to traffic in 1914.

IN THE DOMINICAN REPUBLIC AND HAITI

In 1904, following civil war, the Dominican Republic was bankrupt. Rumor had it that Germany and other European countries with investments there might intervene. This led to what is known as the Roosevelt Corollary to the Monroe Doctrine. "Chronic wrongdoing, . . ." said Theodore Roosevelt, "may in America, as elsewhere, ultimately require intervention by some civilized nation." Under the Monroe Doctrine, he concluded, the United States might be forced to exercise "an international police power." In other words, intervention by the United States was justified in order to prevent more damaging intervention by other nations. The United States took over the collection of the Dominican Republic's customs duties and straightened out that nation's debt.

Haiti, which along with the Dominican Republic occupies the island of Hispaniola, had a long record of bad government. In 1915 Haiti was in the midst of one of its periodic revolutions. As in the case of the Dominican Republic, the United States feared intervention by Europeans because that might prove detrimental to American interests in Haiti and to United States control of the Panama Canal. So the United States government landed troops in Haiti and assumed control over Haitian affairs. The troops were not withdrawn until 1934.

Since 1934, terror, corruption, and poverty have continued to be common in Haiti. For instance, from 1957 until their ouster in 1986, dictators Dr. Francois Duvalier and his son Jean-Claude pocketed much of the country's wealth. Today's reform-minded government is barely standing against the pressure from Latin American drug traffickers and a power-hungry military.

A CHANGE IN POLICY

Beginning with President Herbert Hoover, the United States moved away from its policy of intervening in Latin American affairs. In 1929, Hoover began pulling troops out of Haiti and Nicaragua. And he refused to intervene in the early 1930s when several Latin American countries were unable to pay debts they owed to American businessmen.

In 1933, President Franklin D. Roosevelt sought to promote hemispheric solidarity by a program known as the Good Neighbor Policy. That year, the United States signed an agreement with other American nations that said, "No state has the right to intervene in the internal or external affairs of another." The next year, the Platt Amendment was repealed.

The change in policy eventually had an effect on the Panama Canal Zone. Beginning in the 1960s, Panamanian demands that the United Staets turn over control of the zone to Panama grew. Finally, meeting in Panama in June 1978, President Jimmy Carter and Panama's head of state, Omar Torrijos Herrera, signed several treaties; and on October 1, 1979, Panama began gradually to take control of the canal and the land around it.

Under the treaties, Panama agreed to pay certain costs involved in transferring the land to Panamanian ownership. That country also agreed that the United States could place the zone under military control if the security of the zone were threatened. Panama would assume full control after December 31, 1999.

In the late 1980s, Panama's ruler, General Manuel Noriega, was almost forced from power by a national strike. Noriega's lack of popularity stemmed from his deals with the U.S. Central Intelligence Agency, from his reputed drug smuggling, and from Panama's high unemployment. Despite the strike, Noriega remained in power.

CREATING AN ORGANIZATION OF AMERICAN STATES

Prior to World War II, the United States intervened in Latin America primarily to protect investments in mines, plantations, and oil fields. Then the Good Neighbor Policy marked a period of nonintervention. After the war, intervention revived, now mainly for the stated purpose of preventing the spread of communism. At the same time, the United States worked to bring about greater cooperation among nations of the Western Hemisphere.

The idea of American nations working together to solve their problems can be traced back to Simón Bolívar's vision of a unified South America. In the years following his unsuccessful struggle, several hemispheric conferences had explored inter-American cooperation. Finally, the Pan American Union was set up in 1910, with headquarters in Washington, D.C. In 1948 the union was renamed the Organization of American States (OAS), and its staff, which had consisted almost exclusively of United States citizens, was broadened to include persons from other nations in the Western Hemisphere. The purpose of the OAS was to provide for hemispheric defense against aggression, both within and without, and to provide a means for dealing cooperatively with political and economic problems.

In the meantime, after World War II, the United States sent more than $25 billion in aid to European countries to help them recover economically and to build up their armed forces as a defense against the Soviet Union. Little aid went to Latin America. In 1958, however, Vice-President Richard M. Nixon ran into anti-United States demonstrations in Peru and Venezuela during a tour of Latin American countries. Following this, Brazil's President Juscelino Kubitschek argued that Latin America's main problem was the deep misery and desperation so many of the region's people experienced. He suggested that the United States do more to help Latin American countries overcome their poverty. And, after meetings between the United States and Latin American officials, the Inter-American Development Bank was established to make loans for this purpose.

THE ALLIANCE FOR PROGRESS

That same year, 1959, Cuba became a Communist nation. United States policymakers feared the establishment of more Communist governments in the Western Hemisphere. This fear spurred the creation of the Alliance for Progress—or *Alianza para el Progreso*—a plan proposed by President John F. Kennedy in 1961 to transform Latin America through the joint efforts of government and private investors.

The Alliance for Progress was a tremendously ambitious program. Over the course of ten years, the expenditure of $100 billion was proposed, 80 percent of which was to be furnished by Latin American nations themselves. Between 1961 and 1969, the United States poured $10.3 billion in aid money into Latin America. Total private investment from United States lenders during that period came to $1.4 billion.

Under the Alliance for Progress, thousands of schools, hospitals, and housing units were built. Schoolchildren received textbooks and free meals. Between 1960 and 1967, thanks at least in part to the Alliance for Progress, the percentage of children aged five to fourteen enrolled in school went from 49.8 to 56.8. About a million families were settled or resettled on land formerly owned by wealthy landowners. Roads, dams, and hydroelectric plants as well as factories were constructed. Many new jobs were created.

Unfortunately, the Alliance for Progress revealed more problems than it solved. Millions still lived in slums or were landless, nearly half of all children remained out of school, and progress made in agriculture production was canceled out by the high birth rate.

By the end of the 1960s the United States economy was sliding into a recession. Congress became more and more reluctant to appropriate money for economic or other aid to foreign countries. The Alliance for progress ended, having fallen far short of the goals that had been set for it.

EL SALVADOR, NICARAGUA, AND GRENADA

Early in 1980 the tiny Central American country of El Salvador was rocked by political violence following the establishment of a joint military-civilian government. In March the much-admired Roman Catholic archbishop Óscar Romero was assassinated while officiating at a Mass. Then in December of 1980 six Americans, including some nurses who were nuns, were killed. Some observers charged that the assassins were in the pay of the Salvadoran regime. Violence has continued. U.S. military advisers have helped the Salvadoran government while Cuban, Soviet, and Nicaraguan support has aided the rebels.

In nearby Nicaragua in 1979, rebels overthrew General Anastasio Somoza, whose family

had ruled Nicaragua as dictators for forty-five years. The rebels, called Sandinistas, set up a socialist government. An antigovernment group, the *contras*, used intermittent U.S. aid to fight the Sandinistas. In the spring of 1988, the Nicaraguan government and the *contras* negotiated an uneasy ceasefire and began peace talks.

The United States also opposed the socialist government of the Caribbean island of Grenada and its growing Soviet-Cuban ties. In October 1983, U.S. troops invaded Grenada and overthrew its government. A year later a democratic government was reestablished.

PUERTO RICO

Some observers have regarded Latin American countries, especially those in the Caribbean Sea and in Central America, as practically colonies of the United States. But, with the exception of Puerto Rico, none ever was a United States dependency, however close their political and economic ties. Puerto Rico, formerly a Spanish possession, was ceded to the United States as bounty of the Spanish-American War of 1898.

The United States funded school and hospital construction and set up a program of medical care. It brought electricity to the island, and installed a telephone and telegraph system as well. American corporations invested in sugar and tobacco acreage. What had been small, individually owned farm holdings gave way to large plantations, most of them held by absentee owners. The number of landless peasants and occasional laborers who earned only three dollars a week rose accordingly. Puerto Rico produced wealth, but little of it flowed to the people themselves. In 1940 the average annual income for Puerto Ricans was only $121. Sugar, tobacco, and practically everything else Puerto Ricans produced were sold to the United States, and that country supplied nearly all of Puerto Rico's manufactured goods.

At first the United States ruled the island through a military government that remained in control for twenty months. In 1900 the United States granted Puerto Rico a constitution under which Puerto Ricans could elect a legislature. They could also elect one person to represent them, but without a vote, in the United States House of Representatives. The President of the United States appointed a governor to head the island's government and a council of five Puerto Ricans and six United States citizens to advise the governor. In 1917 Congress made all Puerto Ricans citizens of the United States.

The United States sought to establish the American way of life in Puerto Rico. Although all Puerto Ricans continued to speak Spanish, all students were required to study English in school. Textbooks, printed in English, were imported. American cars appeared on city streets and in the countryside. In time, all Puerto Ricans even had social security numbers.

In 1946, President Harry S Truman appointed the first native governor of Puerto Rico, Jesús T. Piñero. The following year Puerto Ricans were given the right to elect their governor. In 1952, after approving a constitution written by a Puerto Rican convention, the island became a commonwealth, able to govern all its domestic affairs. Foreign relations and defense, however, continued to be handled by the United States.

Puerto Ricans have no vote in Congress and they do not pay federal income taxes, but they have been subject to the draft. The majority political party, the Popular Democrats, supports continued commonwealth status for the island. The New Progressive party, which favors statehood, has been gaining support in recent years and today represents about 40 to 45 percent of the population. A tiny Independence party has attracted fewer than 5 percent of the people.

Under Governor Luis Muñoz Marín, the Puerto Rican government in the 1950s launched "Operation Bootstrap," a program mainly concerned with drawing more American companies to Puerto Rico. To attract investors, the plan exempted new manufacturers from taxation for ten years. Between 1950 and 1968, some seventeen hundred new industrial plants employing more than 100,000 workers were established there. They turned out clothing, textiles, petroleum products, chemicals, and many other goods. Average income on the island, which had been $297 in 1950, rose to $3,900 in 1983. A new middle class was created.

In addition, during the 1960s the United States declared Cuba off limits to American citizens. Much of the huge tourist business Cuba had enjoyed shifted to Puerto Rico. In 1970 1.5 million tourists visited the island.

As in many other countries during the 1970s, Puerto Rico has suffered economic setbacks. Puerto Rico has to import oil to run its industry, and the tripling of world oil prices in 1973 raised the cost of goods produced on the island. In addition, clothing and textile sales dropped as buyers turned to Hong Kong, Taiwan, and South Korea, where textile prices were lower and workers received lower wages than in Puerto Rico.

Unemployment also remained high on the island because of population growth. Improved health care brought a drop in the death rate, causing the population to soar from 1.8 million in 1940 to 3.2 million in 1980. During the postwar period about a million Puerto Ricans migrated to the mainland. The majority of them settled in New York City. Thousands of others now live in Chicago, Detroit, Milwaukee, Newark, Philadelphia, and Los Angeles. To accommodate children of Puerto Rican immigrants as well as Spanish-speaking students, classes in many public school systems are taught in Spanish.

CONFRONTING CURRENT PROBLEMS

In a society that provides economic opportunity, poor people have a chance to improve their lot in life. At least, thanks to their efforts, their children and grandchildren might be better off, receive a better education, and have greater job opportunities.

But in Latin America, economic and social betterment escapes the grasp of millions of people. There simply are not enough jobs for everyone. Job-producing investment—to build factories and so forth—remains woefully short.

Although Mexico, Venezuela, Peru, and some other nations have increased their share of ownership in various industries, around 75 percent of investment in Latin America remains under foreign control. A large portion of the annual profits of both foreign and domestic investors continues to flow out of the region, instead of being invested for the benefit of Latin Americans.

The need for investment capital is but one of Latin America's economic problems. Land reform is frequently regarded as another needed step toward the overall development of many countries. Most land in Latin America continues to remain in the hands of the few. Landowners by and large have hired laborers to work the land at low wages and have not made it possible for workers to buy land for themselves. There have been some land distribution programs—in Mexico, Venezuela, Bolivia, Chile, Colombia, and Peru. But on the whole, progress has been very slow.

The poor, both urban and rural, are born into poverty and in that state they die. And so do their children. Moreover, thanks to ever-increasing population, the ranks of the Latin American poor and landless swell every day.

AMONG THE INDIANS OF ECUADOR

What does it mean to be poor and landless? Many Latin Americans who know are Indians, a people for the most part exploited and discriminated against.

Some descendants of the Incas in Ecuador once made a film about a typical market day, called "Our Lives." This is the sound track:

This dark room is where we live. We have nothing but a reed door between two mud walls. It is a poor little house.

Here are our crops and our animals. This is all that we have. We have no pasture for our burro, for our cow, for our sheep.

Our house is the same as the houses of

Opposite: Pedestrians and vehicles choke a narrow street in an old section of Quito, Ecuador. One of Pizarro's lieutenants founded Quito on the embers of an Inca capital.

our neighbors, with a roof made of grass. Here we live with our families and form our community.

The community where we live in our small huts is surrounded by mud walls to protect our crops and animals. In all the *campos* [lands or fields] of our Ecuador, we speak only our language *Quechua*.

All of these communities are far from the city, from the capital of the *cantón* [province]. Around our houses are only our little plots of land. The large fields belong to the *patrón* [owner of the estate].

Here is another community, also of Indian people. We Indians are in the majority in the cantón and in the entire country. Majority means that there are more Indians than *blancos* [whites].

Large fields of barley grow, but little of it is ours.

These are beautiful heads of barley, our food and the food of our children, which we grow with great care.

The most delicious food is prepared from the *quinoa* [a weedy plant; the ground seeds are used as a cereal]. It is the plant of our ancestors, the Incas, who lived here before the Spaniards came. Over these paths we walk barefoot, carrying animals and grain long distances.

The footpaths lead to the road. On it men and women go to the town, to the market to sell our animals and crops. *Campesinos* [peasants] who have no money cannot go in the bus; most of us go on foot.

On the road run the buses. Many of the drivers are not responsible. They run over people and animals. They carry many people, even on top and hanging to the back, at the risk of their lives. Those who have money go by bus. It is in the bus that the mistreatment of the campesino begins.

We go to the market. The *cholos* [mestizo merchants] and hucksters start taking ad-

vantage of us. They buy our products at low prices.

Many people of the campo go to buy and sell. We are cheated by a few cunning merchants. The cholos abuse the campesinos. This is the place, the people, the market, where illegal taxes are collected.

We have no way to entertain ourselves. We have no movies. We don't know how to play ball. We have only the *chicheria* [bar] to enjoy ourselves with our friends, when we spend our money and enrich the owner.

We are all kinds of people, from all parts of the country. We are poor. We have no power in the government. The government is not of the campesino.

We live in misery and sorrow.

Many people sell their grain at the market. The buyers rob us with unfair measures and weights. The hucksters are those who get all of our grain and then sell it back at raised prices when we don't have any.

This is the animal market where also there is no lack of cheaters. Where many taxes are unfairly collected from the campesino because he doesn't know the laws. Because of this we have to learn the laws and how to defend ourselves.

Many buyers, cholos, and traders abuse the campesinos by taking their money against their will.

Has this happened to you? . . . When they pay us less than our animals are worth, what can we do?

Our women sell their little handworks, like sashes and braidings, but they don't bring in anything, nobody pays much. Why aren't our products worth anything? But the blancos sell many things at high prices. They sell ponchos, shirts, pants, cloth, thread, and other things. Why can't we, too, sell the same things at our own markets?

Why don't we have money to buy things that we don't have, like this water pond?

They make us leave, dirty and unwashed.

In the cantón capital they have plenty of water. They have public health service. We don't even have light. All we have is a little candle, this weak little flame. The blancos have electric light which works in the night. The campesino doesn't have any, we live in the dark at night.

In the cantón are services of the center of public health. There are drugstores, there are schools, there are decorated plazas and the large buildings of the municipality. The campesinos don't have services like drugstores, like the people in the cantón capital have.

The campesino has no money. He goes to the money-lenders to borrow. The campesinos don't know the laws. They go to the lawyers to get justice. But the lawyers cheat him and don't work for justice, but rather for money. They don't make justice for the campesinos.

Our church ought to teach love, charity, and justice, but it doesn't. The people are dying of their hunger for these things. They are sad because they're not taught.

The municipality has many employees. But they don't care about the campesinos. The employees know how to collect taxes without authority, even though they get their own salaries.

Brothers, why don't we too have the things that the cholos and blancos have? This is our land, we were Ecuadorians before anyone else. From now on we must all get together and talk about how we can work to get what we want.

DISSENT AND SUPPRESSION

Without a tradition of orderly protest and the right to disagree, many Latin American countries have handled dissent in ways that have led to violence.

Often government efforts to suppress dissent have triggered even more violence in reaction, creating a vicious circle of human rights abuses.

Radical groups are not alone in fearing government retaliation for their actions. Numerous individual citizens who protest government actions and policies also find themselves in jail and under torture. Said a news story out of Brazil in the mid-1970s:

A prominent lawyer, Wellington Rocha Cantal, who was arrested in São Paulo on April 3 [1974], has started legal action against the internal defense center for illegal detention and ill treatment. Mr. Cantal charges that he was kept for several days without food and water, hooded, stripped naked, kicked, beaten, suspended by his arms from hooks and given electric shocks.

The Brazilian Bar Association issued a strong protest against the "physical and moral torture" of Mr. Cantal. And in August, when the association held its national conference, several lawyers denounced the practice of torture and called for the return to a "state of law."

Catholic church leaders, most prominent among them the Archbishop of São Paulo, Paulo Evaristo Cardinal Arns, have also protested the continued use of torture in the interrogation of opposition suspects. The torture issue has been the principal cause of strain in church-state relations in this largely Catholic country of 104 million people.

Unfortunately, similar stories are all too common in today's newspapers. They report that both urban guerrillas and rebels in the countryside use kidnappings and assassinations to initiate change or to seize power. The leader of Mexico's oil workers union was arrested in 1989 for possession of more than two hundred weapons in his home. Police officials presume that the arms were to be used to strong-arm the union's way back into power, despite the presence of a new president who has plans to clean up the union corruption.

In Argentina, many children were taken away from their natural parents during the 1977 period of military dictatorship, torture, and murder when 9,000 Argentines suspected of being leftist subversives disappeared. Now those children, most of whom were adopted after being seized, are being located by their relatives and fought over in emotional custody suits.

A particularly brutal incident in 1986 involved a young Chilean man on his way to a protest march against Augusto Pinochet. The young man was stopped by a military patrol truck, beaten, doused with gasoline, and set on fire. He was then tossed on a truck and dumped along a roadside. He later died.

Individuals and groups around the world have persuaded some governments to stop these atrocities simply by reporting the incidents to the world. If the fragile democracies established recently are to stand, they will have to ensure a new tradition of peaceful protest.

OTHER PROBLEMS AND SOLUTIONS

Overpopulation, economic depression, and civil strife are three more problems affecting the future of Latin America. Latin America's population in 1900 was about 62 million. By the middle of the 1980s it exceeded 400 million. Such a population overload places enormous stress on struggling economies. Furthermore, money spent on guns and other war materiel, not to mention the cost of military personnel, diverts scarce resources away from the economy. The result is poverty and discontent.

Many Latin American leaders agree that their countries need to cooperate to solve their problems. They point to regional associations in Western Europe that have reduced trade barriers, cooperated on defense policies, and worked to reduce tensions.

One of the most notable attempts at Latin American cooperation in recent years has been the Arias Peace Plan. In 1987, Oscar Arias Sánchez, president of Costa Rica, proposed a set of resolutions designed to reduce conflict in Central America. In particular, he hoped to end the guerrilla wars in El Salvador and Nicaragua. Arias characterized his plan as the first step in promoting regional efforts to solve the problems of Latin America. Arias won the 1987 Nobel Peace Prize for his plan.

LOOKING AHEAD

Throughout the history of Latin America democracy has played second fiddle to military and other dictatorships. Yet in recent years, several countries—notably Mexico, Brazil, Argentina, Chile, and Grenada—appear to be establishing, or reestablishing, stable, civilian governments that hold honest and meaningful elections. In the end, the Latin American government that provides fair opportunities for its people to have adequate food, clothing, and shelter is the government most likely to survive.

Opposite: Mexican peasants fashion handicrafts of great beauty, such as the *huipil*, or loose blouse, worn by this Mayan woman.

ca. 25,000 B.C.	Human migration from Siberia into Americas
3500–3000 B.C.	Beginning of village life in Central America
1200–100 B.C.	Flourishing of Olmec culture
A.D. 300–900	Flourishing of Mayan culture
1100–1200	Aztec entry into Mexico
ca. 1200	Inca migration into highlands
ca. 1325	Founding of Tenochtitlán
ca. 1400	Beginning of Inca conquests
1440–69	Reign of Aztec emperor Montezuma I
1492–93	First voyage of Christopher Columbus
1493–96	Second voyage of Christopher Columbus
1496	Founding of Santo Domingo
1500	Pedro Álvares Cabral reaches coast of Brazil on voyage to India
1502–20	Reign of Aztec emperor Montezuma II
1504	Hernán Cortés embarks for New World
1510	Francisco Pizarro embarks for Americas
1511	Spanish conquest of Cuba
1513	Vasco Núñez de Balboa discovers and claims the Pacific Ocean for Spain
1519	Cortés lands in Mexico, founds Veracruz, and marches to Tenochtitlán
June 30, 1520	*La Noche Triste*
1521	Spanish complete conquest of Aztecs
ca. 1531	Inca civil war, War of the Brothers
1532	Pizarro reaches Peru and begins Spanish conquest
1533	Execution of Inca ruler Atahualpa
1538–53	Founding of universities in Santo Domingo, Mexico, and Peru
1541	Pizarro assassinated
ca. 1545	Beginning of silver mining at Potosí
1697	French take over Saint-Domingue
1789	French Revolution begins
1791	Slave rebellion in Haiti
1799	Pierre Dominique Toussaint L'Ouverture becomes governor of Haiti
1803	Death of Toussaint in prison
1804	Haiti becomes independent nation
1806	Francisco de Miranda leads unsuccessful uprising against Spain in Venezuela
1810	Miguel Hidalgo y Costilla leads uprising against Spain in Mexico
1811	Hidalgo executed
	Spanish forces again crush uprising in Venezuela
1813	Simón Bolívar leads invasion of Venezuela
1814	José María Morelos declares Mexico independent
1821	Rebels victorious in Venezuela
	Mexico achieves independence
	Bolívar elected president of Gran Colombia
1822	Agustín I becomes emperor of Mexico
	Antonio José de Sucre defeats Spanish in Ecuador
	Brazil declares independence from Portugal
1823	Agustín I overthrown
	Monroe Doctrine formulated
1824	José de San Martin and Bolívar bring independence to Peru
1825	Bolivia becomes an independent nation
1828	Uruguay achieves independence
1830	Death of Bolívar
1831	Dom Pedro I of Brazil abdicates
1833–55	Antonio López de Santa Anna dominates Mexican politics
1835–52	Juan Manuel de Rosas holds power in Argentina
1836	Texas achieves independence from Mexico
1840	Dom Pedro II proclaimed emperor of Brazil
1846–48	Mexican War with the United States
1857	Liberal constitution adopted in Mexico
1858–61	War of the Reform in Mexico
1861	Benito Juárez becomes president of Mexico
1864–67	France attempts to establish a Mexican empire under Archduke Maximilian of Austria
1868–78	Ten Years' War in Cuba
1872	Death of Juárez

1876–1911	Porfirio Díaz holds power in Mexico
1889	Dom Pedro II deposed; Brazil proclaimed a republic
1898	Spanish-American War; Cuba gains independence; Puerto Rico becomes a United States possession
1903	Panama achieves independence
1904	Work begins on Panama Canal
	Theodore Roosevelt announces Roosevelt Corollary
1910	Pan American Union formed
1911	Díaz overthrown in Mexico; Francisco Madero elected president
1913	Victortiano Huerta takes over Mexican government
1914	Huerta overthrown; Venustiano Carranza becomes president of Mexico
	Panama Canal opens
1917	Mexican congress adopts a revolutionary constitution
1920–24	Álvaro Obregón president of Mexico
1924–28	Plutarco Calles president of Mexico
1930	Getulio Vargas becomes president of Brazil
1932	New Chilean constitution goes into effect
1933	Beginning of Good Neighbor Policy
1933–59	Fulgencio Batista holds power in Cuba
1934	Platt Amendment repealed
1938	Mexico seizes foreign oil properties
1943	Army coup topples Argentine government
1946	Juan Perón becomes president of Argentina
1948	Organization of American States formed
1952	Puerto Rico becomes a commonwealth
1954	Vargas commits suicide
1955	Perón government overthrown in Argentina
1956	Juscelino Kubitschek becomes president of Brazil
1959	Fidel Castro overthrows Batista
1960	Brasília dedicated as capital of Brazil
1961	United States breaks diplomatic relations with Cuba; Bay of Pigs incident
	Jânio Quadros becomes president of Brazil, but resigns after seven months; João Goulart becomes president
	Alliance for Progress begins
1962	Cuban missile crisis
1964	Army coup in Brazil overthrows Goulart
	Eduardo Frei Montalva elected president of Chile
1970	Salvador Allende elected president of Chile
1973	Army coup brings Allende government down
	Perón elected Argentine president once more
1974	Death of Juan Perón; his widow, Isabel Perón, becomes president of Argentina
1976	Military junta ousts Isabel Perón
1979	Sandinistas overthrow General Anastasio Somoza in Nicaragua
1982	Falkland Islands War
1983	Raúl Alfonsín elected President of Argentina
	U.S. troops invade Grenada
1988	Peace talks begin between *contras* and Nicaraguan government

Schools of practical learning shaped by the goals of the Revolution are depicted in this Diego Rivera mural.

INDEX AND GLOSSARY

As an aid to the reader, definitions of many Latin American terms are included in this Index and Glossary.

Persons with compound family names are listed according to custom, generally under the name that follows their given name. For example: Salvador Allende Gossens *is found under* Allende.

ACKNOWLEDGMENTS

Bantam Books Inc.: For material from the film *Cashnami Nucanchijpaj Causai* by Manuel Bagua et al. appearing in *Latin America Yesterday and Today* edited by John Rothchild; copyright © 1973 by Bantam Books Inc. E. P. Dutton & Co., Inc.: For material from *Child of the Dark, The Diary of Carolina Maria de Jesus* translated by David St. Clair; copyright © 1962 by E. P. Dutton & Co., Inc. and Souvenir Press Ltd. For material from *In Praise of Darkness* by Jorge Luis Borges, translated by Norman Thomas de Giovanni; copyright © 1969-74 by Emece Editores S.A. and Norman Thomas de Giovanni. Holt, Rinehart and Winston, Inc.: For material from *San Pedro, Colombia: Small Town in a Developing Society* by Miles Richardson; copyright © 1970 by Holt, Rinehart and Winston, Inc. For material from *The Forgotten Frontier: Ranchers of North Brazil* by Peter Rivière; copyright © 1972 by Holt, Rinehart and Winston, Inc. For material from *The Zinacantecos of Mexico: A Modern Maya Way of Life* by Evon Z. Vogt; copyright © 1970 by Holt, Rinehart and Winston, Inc. Indiana University Press: For "Fear" by Gabriela Mistral; from *Selected Poems of Gabriela Mistral* translated by Langston Hughes; copyright © 1957 by Indiana University Press. Stanley Meisler: For material from "Cuba" from *The Atlantic Monthly;* copyright © 1975 by The Atlantic Monthly Company, Boston, Mass. New Directions Publishing Corp.: For excerpts from "Brazil" by Ronald de Carvalho, translated by Dudley Poore, and "The Indians Come Down from Mixco" by Miguel Angel Asturias, translated by Donald D. Walsh; from *Anthology of Contemporary Latin-American Poetry* edited by Dudley Fitts; copyright 1942, 1947 by New Directions Publishing Corp. Newsweek, Inc.: For material from "How Brazil Flies With Inflation"; copyright 1973 by Newsweek, Inc. For material from "Down in the Dumps"; copyright 1974 by Newsweek, Inc. The New Yorker: For material from "Letter From Santiago" by Joseph Kraft; © 1971 by The New Yorker Magazine, Inc. The New York Times: For material from *The New York Times;* © 1974 by The New York Times Company. Praeger Publishers, Inc.: For material from *The Latin Americans* by Victor Alba; © 1969 by Praeger Publishers, Inc. Frederick Ungar Publishing Co., Inc.: For "The Flamingos' Stockings" by Horacio Quiroga, translated by W. P. Negron and W. K. J. from *Spanish-American Literature in Translation: A Selection of Poetry, Fiction, and Drama since 1888* edited by Willis Knapp Jones; copyright © 1963 by Frederick Ungar Publishing Co., Inc. The University of Michigan Press: For material from *The View from the Barrio* by Lisa Redfield Peattie; © 1968 by The University of Michigan Press. The University of Pennsylvania Press: For "She Who Understands" by Alfonsina Storni, from *Some Spanish-American Poets* edited by Alice Stone Blackwell, 1937. D. Van Nostrand Company: For material from *Contemporary Latin America* by L. Hanke; © 1968 by Litton Educational Publishing, Inc. The New York Times: For material from "At an Argentine Party After the Coup" from *The New York Times;* © 1976 by The New York Times Company. For "Lazybones" from *We Are Many* by Pablo Neruda, translated by Alastair Reid; copyright © 1967-70 by Cape Goliard Press, Ltd., reprinted by permission of Grossman Publishers. The authors and editors have made every effort to trace the ownership of all copyrighted selections found in this book and to make full acknowledgment for their use.

ILLUSTRATIONS

Jean-Marc Tingaud, cover; Armin Haab, from *Mexico,* Reich Verlag, Lucerne, 2; Dumbarton Oaks, 8; Edward Ranney, 10, 19; Lee Boltin, 12; Staatliche Museen Preussischer Kulturbesitz, West Berlin, Museum für Völkerkunde, 14(left), 28; Museo de América, Madrid, 14(right); Ferdinand Anton, Courtesy Trustees of the British Museum, 15; Ferdinand Anton, Munich, 20; The John Carter Brown Library, Brown University, 22; A. Guillèn, 26; Courtesy OAS, 30, 34, 144; Bradley Smith, 32, 44, 52, 161; Radio Times Hulton Picture Library, 36; Brown Brothers, 37, 56; Hans Mann, Monkmeyer, 42; Georg Gerster, Rapho/Photo Researchers, 48; Franco Cianetti, 49; Courtesy of Visual Arts Unit, OAS, Washington, D.C., 62; Courtesy, Girard Foundation, 64, 68; Courtesy, Bernard S. Myers, 65; Cornell Capa, Magnum, 72, 130, 152, 159; P. J. Menzel, Stock, Boston, 75; Michael Friedel, 76; Eugen Kusch, *Mexico in Pictures,* © 1968, Verlag Hans Carl, Nuremberg, 80; Fulvio Roiter, 84, 112–113, 115; P. G. Rivière from *The Forgotten Frontier: Ranchers of North Brazil* by Peter Rivière, © 1972 by Holt, Rinehart and Winston, Inc. Reproduced by permission of Holt, Rinehart and Winston, 89; John Cohen, 90; Carl Frank, 98, 116, 120; Lisa Redfield Peattie, from *The View from the Barrio,* The University of Michigan Press, © 1968, 102; Werner Muckenhirn, DPI, 105; Leonard McCombe from Time-Life Books Life World Library Series, Time-Life Picture Agency © Time Inc., 110; Howard Sochurek, Woodfin Camp, 114; Peter Scheier, Monkmeyer, 117; G. Petersen, FPG, 118(top); Owen Franken, Stock, Boston, 118(bottom); Marc & Evelyne Bernheim, Woodfin Camp, 119; Lew Merrim, Monkmeyer, 121; Lee Lockwood, Black Star, 122, 129; Stephen Shames, Black Star, 125; Ted Spiegel, Black Star, 133; C. M. Fitch, FPG, 135; Gisele Freund, Magnum, 136; Y. Futagawa, 140; The Bettmann Archive, Inc., 147; Marilyn Silverstone, Magnum, 157; Edward Grazda, Magnum, 158.

Maps executed by Paul Hazelrigg

STUDENT'S GUIDE

LATIN AMERICA

BY M. L. CLARDY

AZTECS AND INCAS

IN THIS CHAPTER YOU WILL DISCOVER:

How the Aztecs organized their societies

Why the Aztecs believed their gods required human sacrifice

How the Incas built their civilization among high mountains in South America

KEY QUESTIONS

1. Describe the Aztec city, Tenochtitlán. What were some unusual and impressive features of this city?

2. How far did Aztec rule extend? What was the relationship between the Aztecs and their subject peoples?

3. What Aztec characteristics did a Spanish observer note? Describe the appearance of the Aztecs.

4. How did the Aztecs choose their ruler? What special privileges did he have?

5. Outline the organization of social classes in Aztec society. What determined an individual's class? Describe some of the skills required of craftsmen and farmers.

6. Explain why, although the Aztecs knew the principle of the wheel, they did not use it in transportation. What difference might using the wheel have made to their society?

7. Why was religion important in the daily lives of the Aztecs? What purpose did religious ceremony serve? Why did the Aztecs believe that their gods required human sacrifice?

8. Where did the Incas live? Why, according to Inca legend, did they live there? Indicate ways in which this location influenced the Inca way of life.

9. Describe the special practices which reinforced the Inca belief that the Sapa Inca was related to a god. Why did the Sapa Inca take part in a planting ceremony?

10. What problems did the Incas face in building a transportation and communication network? Explain how these problems were solved.

11. What resources did the Incas depend on for food? How did

IMPORTANT PEOPLE

Montezuma I
   (Mon-tay-'zoo-mah)

Montezuma II

Sapa Inca ('Sah-pah 'Een-kah)

Huayna Capac (Oo-'ī-nah
   'Kah-pahk)

Atahualpa (Ah-tah-'wahl-pah)

Huáscar (Oo-'ahs-kar)

IMPORTANT WORDS AND CONCEPTS

maize (mayz)

Maya ('My-uh)

Olmecs ('Ahl-mex)

Aztecs

Yucatán Peninsula
   (Yoo-kah-'tahn)

Tenochtitlán (Teh-nok-teet-'lahn)

calpulli (kahl-'poo-lee)

peasants

slavery

slash-and-burn agriculture

Huitzilopochtli
   (Wheet-zee-loh-'pokt-lee)

Quetzalcoatl (Ket-'sahl-kwaht-l)

human sacrifice

Cuzco ('Kooz-koh)

Quito ('Kee-toh)

War of the Brothers

the peasants contribute to the provision of food for all the Incas?

12. List some of the conditions that weakened the Inca empire.

Chapter 2 THE SEARCH FOR EL DORADO

IN THIS CHAPTER YOU WILL DISCOVER:

Why Spanish explorers risked their lives and fortunes to conquer the New World

How certain Aztec beliefs made the Spanish invasion easier

Why Roman Catholic priests accompanied the expeditions

How the Spanish changed the Mexican way of life

KEY QUESTIONS

1. Explain the system of encomienda that the Spaniards brought to the Americas. Were Indians held in encomienda actually enslaved?

2. The Spanish exploration of Latin America is said to have been inspired by a desire for gold and glory and opportunity to serve God. Give examples of Spanish explorers and adventurers who demonstrate one or more of these motives.

3. Several Spanish explorers endured a hard life and died in disgrace, in despair, or from violence resulting from disagreements. What caused these harsh conditions? What were the long range contributions of these explorers?

4. What aspects of Aztec technology and religion helped to make the Spanish conquest under Cortés possible?

5. List at least three reasons Spanish Roman Catholics may have used to justify converting Indians.

6. What issues caused the friction between Cortés and Diego Velázquez? Why would these create problems for the Spanish conquest?

7. In what respect did the Spanish ignorance of Aztec customs create problems? What were the events of la Noche Triste?

8. The Spanish held several advantages over the Aztecs. How

IMPORTANT PEOPLE

Christopher Columbus

Juan Ponce de León (Hwahn 'Pon say day Lay-'ohn)

Álvar Núñez Cabeza de Vaca ('Ahl vahr 'Noo-nyez Kah-'bay-sah day 'Vah-kah)

Francisco Coronado (Frahn-'sees-koh Kor-oh-'nah-doh)

Hernando de Soto (Er-'nahn-doh day 'So-toh)

Hernán Cortés (Er-'nahn Kor-'tes)

Cuitláhuac (Koo-eet-'lah-hoo-ahk)

IMPORTANT WORDS AND CONCEPTS

Santo Domingo ('Sahn-toh Doh-'meen-go)

encomienda (en-koh-'myen-dah)

El Dorado (El Doh-'rah-doh)

la Noche Triste (lah 'Noh-chay 'Trees-tay)

3

did reinforcements from Spain make victory possible? What other factors did the Spanish have in their favor?

9. Try to imagine, from the point of view of the Aztecs, the time from the appearance of Cortés to the end of the Aztec surrender on August 13, 1521. Write a brief account of these events from the point of view of an Aztec youth. How would you explain the events which took place?

10. The text indicates that Cortés demonstrated skill as a governor. Give some specific examples that would support this view.

11. Why do you think present-day Mexicans do not feel Cortés was a hero? Evaluate his achievements.

Chapter 3 PIZARRO GAINS AN EMPIRE

IN THIS CHAPTER YOU WILL DISCOVER:

How a legend brought Spaniards to South America

Why the Inca empire fell to Spaniards

KEY QUESTIONS

1. What legend lured Spanish explorers into South America? How did Cortés' experience in Mexico contribute to belief in the legend?

2. How did Pizarro trick Atahualpa? Why did the Spaniards believe that they had to kill the Sapa Inca?

3. Why did Atahualpa accept conversion to Christianity?

4. How did Pizarro die? What benefits did he receive from his exploration?

IMPORTANT PEOPLE

Vasco Núñez de Balboa
('Vahz-koh 'Noo-nyez day Bal-'boh-ah)

Francisco Pizarro
(Frahn-'sees-koh Pee-'zahr-oh)`

IMPORTANT WORDS AND CONCEPTS

Cajamarca (Kah-ha-'mar-kah)

Chapter 4 VICEREGAL RULE AND REVOLUTIONS

IN THIS CHAPTER YOU WILL DISCOVER:

What the social class arrangement was like in the Spanish colonies in Latin America

IMPORTANT PEOPLE

Pedro Alvares Cabral ('Pay-droh 'Ahl-vah-race Kah-'brahl)

Why the Roman Catholic church wielded so much influence

Factors that caused the colonists to revolt against the mother country

How the various colonies gained their independence

KEY QUESTIONS

1. What group made the laws for the Spanish colonies?

2. List the social classes in the Spanish colonies in order of their power. What qualified a person to belong to a certain class?

3. Many Indians died as a result of Spanish colonization. Why?

4. How did the Catholic church react to the Spanish colonists' treatment of Indians and blacks?

5. What roles did the church fulfill in the Spanish colonies? How were the various services of the church financed?

6. Contrast the White Legend and the Black Legend as evaluations of the Spanish conquest. In which ways did the Spanish demonstrate beliefs and practices common to all Europeans of that time?

7. How did Spain benefit from the colonization and exploration of Latin America?

8. Describe the life-style and values found on the estates in Mexico and in boomtowns like Potosí.

9. What event led the Portuguese to settle Brazil? When did this settlement begin?

10. Contrast the Portuguese settlements in Brazil with the Spanish settlements in terms of religion, economy, work force, wealth, and classes of society.

11. Which Latin Americans first gained independence?

12. In what ways were the social structures of Saint-Domingue similar to the social structures of the Spanish colonies?

13. How did the French Revolution contribute to the independence of Saint-Domingue?

14. Describe the successful tactics of Pierre Dominique Toussaint L'Ouverture in defeating the French. How did the French commissioner Sonthonax aid Toussaint's cause?

15. How did Jean Jacques Dessalines's victory contribute to Haiti's poverty?

Thomé de Sousa (Thow-'may day Soh-zah)

Pierre Dominique Toussaint L'Ouverture (Pee-air Doh-mee-neek Too-sahn Loo-vair-tyoor)

Jean Jacques Dessalines (Zhahn Zhahk Des-sah-leen)

Simón Bolívar (See-'mohn Boh-'lee-vahr)

José de San Martín (Hoh-'say day Sahn Mar-'teen)

Miguel Hidalgo y Costilla (Mee-'gehl Ee 'dahl-go ee Kohs-'tee-yah)

José María Morelos (Hoh-'say Mah-'ree-ah Mor-'ay-lohs)

Agustín de Iturbide (Ah-goo-'steen day Ee-toor-'bee-day)

IMPORTANT WORDS AND CONCEPTS

Royal and Supreme Council of the Indies

viceroys

captains-general

peninsulares (pay-neen-soo-'lah-race)

criollos (kree-'oh-yohs)

mestizos (mays-'tee-zohs)

Indians

Black Legend

White Legend

vaqueros (vah-'kay-rohs)

llaneros (yah-'nay-rohs)

gauchos ('gau-chohs)

Potosí (Poh-toh-'see)

16. What forces contributed to other revolutions in Latin America?

17. Why did Simón Bolívar campaign for Gran Colombia after he defeated the Spanish? What caused the defeat of his plan?

18. Compare the careers of Miguel Hidalgo y Costilla and José María Morelos. Describe their goals, methods, and successes and failures. How did these men who were defeated by the Spanish contribute to eventual Mexican independence?

vale un Potosí ('bah-lay oon Poh-toh-'see)

boomtown

grands blancs (grahn blahn)

petits blancs (peh-tee blahn)

gens de couleur (zhahn duh koo-lehr)

French Revolution

Les Amis des Noirs (Lays Ah-mee day Nwahr)

Gran Colombia (Grahn Koh-'lohm-bee-ah)

Chapter 5 POLITICAL TURMOIL

IN THIS CHAPTER YOU WILL DISCOVER:

How the treatment of slaves and Indians differed in Latin America

What roles the church played after independence

Some special characteristics of Latin American politics

Why latifundism hurts the economy

Ways in which foreign investment supports conservative politics

KEY QUESTIONS

1. List the ways in which Spanish treatment of slaves and Indians differed. Why was slavery abolished so quickly?

2. How did the revolutions for independence affect the status of the Roman Catholic church?

3. Discuss Latin American political values. How did Latin Americans select their leaders? What personal characteristics seemed necessary to caudillos?

4. Compare the ideal of Latin American politics with the reality of actual experience in government.

5. What was the spiritual role of the Roman Catholic church?

IMPORTANT WORDS AND CONCEPTS

caudillo (kau-'dee-yoh)

macho ('mah-choh)

golpe de estado ('gohl-pay day ay-'stah-doh)

spiritual and temporal roles of the church

liberals

conservatives

latifundia (lah-tee-'foon-dee-ah)

latifundism (lah-tee-'foon-dizm)

hacendados (hah-sen-'dah-dohs)

haciendas (hah-see-'en-dahs)

estancieros (ay-stahn-see-'ay-rohs)

estancias (ay-'stahn-see-ahs)

middle class

What was the temporal role of the church? How did the church become involved in politics?

6. Why did many Latin Americans oppose the church's participation in politics? Explain the reasons why many mestizos became liberal. Why was the church a central issue between liberals and conservatives?

7. List the economic problems the system of latifundism created.

8. What was the relationship between tenant farmers and latifundists? Why were mestizos more affected by this condition than Indians?

9. Explain why foreign investors in Latin America supported the conservatives. Why didn't these investors produce consumer goods for the Latin Americans?

10. What economic problems resulted from foreign investment?

11. Discuss the reasons why wealthy Latin Americans tended not to invest their money in industry.

Chapter 6 # MEXICO, GROWTH PANGS OF A NATION

IN THIS CHAPTER YOU WILL DISCOVER:

How the Mexican people made heros of two very different leaders—Santa Anna and Juárez

What benefits liberal reform brought to Mexico, and some of the controversy and upheaval that followed

How foreign business interests have influenced Mexican politics

Which groups of Mexicans opposed the Revolution

The division between liberals and conservatives that exists in Mexico today

KEY QUESTIONS

1. What provisions of the Mexican constitution created a weak central government? How did these conditions produce instability?

IMPORTANT PEOPLE

Antonio López de Santa Anna ('Loh-pez day 'Sahn-tah 'Ahn-nah)

Benito Juárez (Bay-'nee-toh 'Hwah-rez)

Napoleon III

Archduke Maximilian

Porfirio Díaz (Por-'fee-ree-oh 'Dee-ahs)

Francisco Madero (Frahn-'sees-koh Mah-'day-roh)

Doroteo Arango/Pancho Villa (Doh-roh-'tay-oh Ah-'rahn-goh/ 'Pahn-choh 'Vee-yah)

Victoriano Huerta (Veek-tor-ee-'ah-noh 'Hwehr-tah)

2. Why did the Mexicans encourage United States citizens to settle in Texas? What bases of disagreement did these settlers have with Mexico? How did the independence of Texas affect Mexico?

3. Discuss the liberals' reason for enacting the Ley Lerdo. Why didn't the law work as they had planned?

4. What provisions in the new Constitution of 1857 caused the War of the Reform? Who fought on the liberal side? Who fought with the conservatives? In what ways did Benito Juárez attempt to support liberal attitudes toward the church?

5. Describe why the War of the Reform resulted in foreign intervention in Mexico. How did United States influence help to bring about the end of Maximilian's rule in Mexico?

6. What methods did Porfirio Díaz use to bring peace and modernization to Mexico? Indicate some of the ways in which Mexicans paid for this peace through loss of freedom. Why did the Yaqui Indians suffer particular hardship?

7. How did *La Sucesión Presidencial en 1910* and Pancho Villa help bring Díaz's rule to an end? Discuss the problems Francisco Madero and Victoriano Huerta faced.

8. What were the provisions of the Constitution of 1917? How did Álvaro Obregón and Plutarco Calles use urban and rural laborers to support this constitution?

9. Describe the land reform program following the Revolution. What were the basic goals of this reform? What problems did land reform produce?

10. Who opposed the Revolution?

11. Why did United States investors become uneasy about the Revolution? What finally caused the takeover of foreign oil companies?

12. How did the Revolution affect the class structure in Mexico?

13. Discuss the ways in which the PRI organized the political life of Mexico. What are some criticisms of this one-party system?

14. How was the 1988 presidential election unusual?

Venustiano Carranza
(Ben-oo-'styah-noh
Kah-'rahn-sah)

Alvaro Obregón ('Ahl-vah-roh
Oh-bray-'gohn)

Plutarco Calles (Ploo-'tahr-koh
'Kah-yays)

Diego Rivera (Dee-'ay-go Ree-'veh-rah)

Lázaro Cárdenas ('Lah-zah-roh
'Kar-day-nahs)

Luis Echeverría Alvarez ('Loo-ees
Ay-cheh-ver-'ee-ah 'Ahl-vah-rez)

José Lopez Portillo
(Hoh-'zay 'Loh-pehz Por-'tee-yoh)

Miguel de la Madrid Hurtado
(Mih-'gel deh lah Mah-'dreed
Hoor-'tah-doh)

Cuauhtémoc Cárdenas
(Qua-'tay-mahk 'Kar-day-nahs)

IMPORTANT WORDS AND CONCEPTS

pronunciamiento
(pro-'noon-see-ah-mee-in-toh)

Nueces River (Noo-ay-says)

Río Grande ('Ree-oh 'Grahn-day)

Ley Lerdo (Lay 'Lehr-doh)

Constitution of 1857

Three Years War/War of the Reform

guardias rurales (gwahr-'dee-ahs
roo-'rah-lays)

ley fuga (lay 'foo-gah)

científico (see-en-'tee-fee-koh)

La Sucesión Presidencial en 1910
(Lah Soo-say-see-'ohn
Pray-see-'den-see-ahl)

Mexican Revolution

Constitution of 1917

Confederación Regional Obrera
Mexicana, CROM
(Kohn-fay-day-rah-see-'ohn
Ray-hee-oh-'nahl Oh-'bray-rah
May-hee-'kah-nah)

Confederación de Trabajadores de Mexico, CTM (Trah-bah-hah-'doh-rays day 'May-hee-koh)

Confederación Nacional de Campesinos (Nah-see-oh-'nahl day Kahm-pay-'see-nohs)

Cristeros (Kree-'stay-rohs)

ejidos (ay-'hee-dohs)

Partido Revolucionario Institucional, PRI (Pahr-'tee-doh Ray-voh-loo-see-oh-'nah-ree-oh Een-stee-too-see-oh-'nahl)

Chapter 7   # GIANTS OF LATIN AMERICAN LITERATURE

IN THIS CHAPTER YOU WILL DISCOVER:

How some Latin American writers have interpreted life in their countries

Some aspects of Latin American literature that demonstrate the ways in which all humans share similar concerns

KEY QUESTIONS

1. What specific items from his everyday life did Pablo Neruda use as subjects in his writing? Indicate ways in which Neruda's stories and poetry point to issues larger than Chile or Latin America.

2. What special concerns of Latin American women do Gabriela Mistral and Alfonsina Storni reveal in their poetry? What evidence do they provide to suggest that the lives of Latin American women differ from those of the men?

3. Describe the special events in the life of Pedro Salvadores which led to his unusual existence for nine years. What motives does Jorge Luis Borges say may have led Salvadores and his wife to maintain this condition? How does Borges indicate that this story has meaning for any and every reader?

4. What values does Borges describe as belonging to the gauchos? In what ways does their life seem separate from

IMPORTANT PEOPLE

Pablo Neruda ('Pah-bloh Nay-'roo dah)

Gabriela Mistral (Gah-bree-'ay-lah Mees-'trahl)

Alfonsina Storni (Ahl-fohn-'see-nah 'Stohr-nee)

Jorge Luis Borges ('Hor-hay 'Loo-ees 'Bor-hays)

Juan Manuel de Rosas (Hwahn Mahn-'wel day 'Roh-sahs)

Miguel Angel Asturias (Mee-'ghel Ahn-'hel Ah-'stoo-ree-ahs)

Horacio Quiroga (Oh-'rah-see-oh Kee-'roh-gah)

Ronald de Carvalho (day Kahr-'vahl-ho)

the lives of other Argentinians? What would motivate a gaucho to become involved in politics? Explain how Borges demonstrates in "The Gauchos" his belief that "any man is all men."

5. In what ways does Miguel Angel Asturias's poem, "The Indians Come Down from Mixco," show an understanding of Indian culture?

6. Indicate why you might recognize "The Flamingos' Stockings" as a Latin American story. What advice does Horacio Quiroga give to readers of this story?

7. What specific Brazilian activities does Ronald de Carvalho speak of? What is his attitude toward Brazil's future?

IMPORTANT WORDS AND CONCEPTS

mazorca (mah-'zohr-kah)

vivas ('bee-bahs)

Chapter 8 **DESCENDANTS OF THE MAYA**

IN THIS CHAPTER YOU WILL DISCOVER:

What daily life is like among the Indians of Zinacantan

How rituals and special days are celebrated

How the Zinacantecos reinforce their sense of community

Ways in which the Zinacantecos combine Spanish and Indian culture

KEY QUESTIONS

1. Compare the daily tasks of Zinacanteco men and women. Why do you think they assign jobs according to sex? How does this practice influence their training during childhood?

2. List the important stages of Zinacanteco life which are marked by ceremonies. What parts of the baptismal ritual promote kinship ties in the society?

3. Describe the courtship practices of the Zinacantecos. What reasons can you give for the involvement of so many people in this ritual? How does this help bind families together?

4. How can Zinacanteco men achieve status through the cargo system? Why are the cargo positions expensive? What services do these men provide for the community?

5. Discuss ways in which the Zinacantecos combine both Span-

IMPORTANT WORDS AND CONCEPTS

municipio (moo-nee-'see-pee-oh)

Zinacantan (Zee-nah-kahn-'tahn)

tortillas (tor-'tee-yahs)

kumpare (koom-'pah-ray)

kumale (koo-'mah-lay)

compadre (kohm-'pah-dray)

comadre (koh-'mah-dray)

Ladinos (Lah-'dee-nohs)

petitioners

brideprice

"house entering"

cargo

Ceremonial Center

mayores (my-'or-ays)

mayordomos (my-or-'doh-mohs)

alféreces (ahl-'fay-ray-says)

regidores (ray-hee-'doh-rays)

ish and Indian culture in their rituals and in their observations of religious holidays.

6. What community involvement occurs when a Zinacanteco dies?

7. What roles do Zinacantecos fill in their local government? What relationship does their local government have with the national government?

8. List the three judgments possible when the presidente and officials attempt to settle disputes.

alcaldes viejos (ahl-'kahl-days bee-'ay-hos)

crèche (cresh)

"soul loss"

sindico ('seen-dee-koh)

cabildo (kah-'beel-doh)

Chapter 9 **IN THE GRASSLANDS OF NORTHERN BRAZIL**

IN THIS CHAPTER YOU WILL DISCOVER:

What special tasks show that a boy of Roraima is becoming an adult

Some of the courtship and marriage customs in Roraima

What daily life is like among the people of Roraima

Why a cattle roundup in northern Brazil is somewhat like a military campaign

IMPORTANT WORDS AND CONCEPTS

Roraima (Raw-'ry-muh)

infant mortality rate

common-law arrangements

vaqueiro (vah-'kay-roh)

fazendeiro (fah-zen-'day-roh)

cafezinho (kah-fay-'zeen-hoh)

siesta (see-'ay-stah)

campeada (kahm-pay-'ah-dah)

KEY QUESTIONS

1. Explain why the people of Roraima wish their children to be baptized as soon after birth as possible.

2. What special tasks mark a boy's life as he moves from age six to adult status? How does the life of a girl in Roraima differ from that of a boy?

3. Why don't some parents in Roraima send their children to school?

4. Describe the courtship and marriage customs in Roraima. Do these rituals have anything in common with the customs of the Zinacantecos?

5. What demands or economic problems grow out of the special conditions of the grasslands? How do the people of Roraima adapt to these conditions?

6. Show how daily life in Roraima is affected by the type of work that the people do.

7. What skills are required by the campeada, the roundup? What purposes do the roundups serve?

8. In what ways has isolation affected the people of Roraima? How might technology change the life of these people?

Chapter 10   THE PEOPLE OF SAN PEDRO, COLOMBIA

IN THIS CHAPTER YOU WILL DISCOVER:

That San Pedro, Colombia, is not a typical peasant village

What leadership roles are available to the men of San Pedro

How small town values influence the daily life and celebrations of its citizens

KEY QUESTIONS

1. What special services does San Pedro provide for its citizens and the citizens of neighboring villages?

2. Using the description of the layout of San Pedro, draw a town map showing the location of the major buildings. Why do you think that church buildings dominate the plaza?

3. Compare the values, social position, wealth, and skills of Don Hernán, Pedro, Don Carlos, Chucho and Don Guido.

4. Explain how the Latin American tradition of male supremacy sometimes differs from reality.

5. What employment is available to Sanpedrano men and women? Why do the factories tend to remain small and relatively lacking in technology? What business problems do Chucho, Mario Tascón, and José Rafael Rojas share?

6. Outline the local government of San Pedro. Indicate whether an official is elected or appointed. In what ways do Sanpedranos view politics as highly personal?

7. What are some of the functions of fiestas in the life of Sanpedranos? Describe the fiesta of the señoritas.

8. What is the relationship of most Sanpedranos to the church?

9. How do the people of San Pedro express their community values in their celebrations? In what way is San Pedro different from a peasant village?

IMPORTANT WORDS AND CONCEPTS

plaza ('plah-zuh)

alcalde (ahl-'kahl-day)

una persona muy formal ('oo-nah pear-'soh-nah mwee fohr-'mahl)

señoritas (seh-nyor-'ee-tahs)

aguinaldos (ah-gee-'nahl-dohs)

pajita emboca (pah-'hee-tah em-'boh-kah)

El Niño de Díos (El 'Nee-nyoh day 'Dee-ohs)

El Día de Los Inocentes (El 'Dee-ah day Lohs Ee-noh-'sahn-tays)

El Día de Los Reyes (El 'Dee-ah day Lohs 'Ray-yays)

toreros (toh-'ray-rohs)

IN THIS CHAPTER YOU WILL DISCOVER:

What some of the problems are for those who live in the barrios of Latin American cities

What school attendance means to children of the barrio

How neighbors in the barrio settle conflicts

What demands are made on people caught in the culture of poverty

How the lives of wealthy Latin Americans differ from those of the poor

KEY QUESTIONS

1. What economic conditions in Venezuela have contributed to the growth of cities like Guayana and barrios such as La Laja? How do the characteristics of the people of La Laja differ from those of the inhabitants of small villages and towns?

2. Barrio children can rarely contribute to the family income. Why does their school attendance present economic problems to their families? Compare factors such as school attendance, curriculum, and teaching methods in your school with those in La Laja.

3. Explain the motivation for attending school that a child in La Laja might have. Would you agree that you have similar motivation for attending school?

4. What examples can you cite which demonstrate that residents of La Laja follow styles or trends? What encourages these people to do so?

5. You have examined the importance of kinship ties among other segments of the Latin American peoples. How does life in the barrio decrease the need for and the possibility of large numbers of kin relationships?

6. In what way does the highly individualized and personalized life-style of the barrio make social relations difficult? How does this difficulty interfere with the settling of conflicts in La Laja? Give specific examples from Peattie's study to support your answer.

IMPORTANT PEOPLE

Lisa Redfield Peattie

Carolina Maria de Jesus
(Kah-roh-'lee-nah Mah-'ree-ah day Hay-'soos)

IMPORTANT WORDS
AND CONCEPTS

Guayana (Gwuh-'yah-nuh)

barrios (bah-'ree-ohs)

La Laja (Lah 'Lah-hah)

clase obrero ('klah-say oh-'breh-roh)

kinship ties

personalized society

haciendo patria (hah-see-'en-doh 'pah-tree-ah)

haciendo pueblo (hah-see-'en-doh) poh-'ay-bloh)

campesinos (kahm-pay-'see-nohs)

favelado, -a (fah-bay-'lah-doh)

Child of the Dark

pepenadores (peh-pen-ah-'doh-rays)

7. How did the development of the barrio council point toward an improvement in community action for La Laja?

8. Why does haciendo patria or haciendo pueblo require the presence of opportunities for each new generation? What makes haciendo patria especially important for citizens of La Laja?

9. Carolina Maria de Jesus' book, *Child of the Dark*, shows the life of someone in "the culture of poverty." What particular demands did she face each day? What values does she express in her diary? What problems do the favelados present for Brazil?

10. Give some examples that show the Mexican government's concern with better conditions for the penenadores. Why does the penenadore seem to prefer not to change?

11. Since the wealthy Argentinians have no need to worry about food and shelter, what concerns do they express? What values do they seem to possess?

Chapter 12 **CUBA**

IN THIS CHAPTER YOU WILL DISCOVER:

How Cuba's independence movement differed from that of other Latin American nations

Why the dictatorships that followed Cuba's independence did little for the people

How the relationship between the United States and Cuba has changed

How different observers interpret the effects of Castro's revolution

KEY QUESTIONS

1. Why did Cubans at first have little interest in gaining their independence from Spain?

2. What goal did Narciso López have in invading Cuba? Why did his expeditions fail?

IMPORTANT PEOPLE

Narciso López
(Nahr-'see-soh 'Loh-pes)

Carlos Manuel de Céspedes
('Kar-lohs mahn-'wel day 'Say-spay-dace)

José Martí y Perez (Hoh-'say Mahr-'tee ee 'Pay-race)

Gerardo Machado
(Gehr-'ahr-doh Ma-'chah-doh)

Fulgencio Batista
(Fool-'hen-see-oh Buh-'tees-tuh)

Fidel Castro (Fee-'dehl 'Kahs-troh)

3. Discuss the attempts of Carlos Manuel de Céspedes and José Martí y Perez to make Cuba independent. Aside from freedom from Spain, what did they hope to achieve?

4. List some ways in which attitudes and events in the United States influenced Cuba's rebellion against Spain. How did American newspapers heighten United States interest in Cuba? Why were the New York *Journal* and *World* encouraged to emphasize stories about Cuba?

5. What did Spain offer the Cuban revolutionaries if they would stop the rebellion? Why did they refuse the offer?

6. Why did President William McKinley order the *Maine* to Cuba? How did this bring the United States into active participation in the rebellion? What did the United States receive for its participation in Cuba's war for independence?

7. Describe the relationship between Cuba and the United States following the enactment of the Platt Amendment. What benefits did Cuba receive? What advantages did the United States obtain?

8. Although the Cuban constitution provided for a democracy, what characteristics did Cuban government display following independence? How was corruption a factor in the government of Cuba?

9. In what ways was the early rebellion of Fidel Castro similar to that of Céspedes? Which segment of Cuban society approved of Castro? How did new methods of communication improve Castro's chances of success?

10. Which of Castro's economic policies caused the United States to boycott Cuban sugar? Describe the characteristics of the Cubans who left Cuba for the United States. What problems did the departure of these people create for the new Cuban government?

11. How did the Bay of Pigs episode and the Cuban missile crisis demonstrate the concern in the United States over Castro's relationship with the Soviet Union?

12. In what ways have the lives of Cubans improved under Castro? What economic problems does Cuba face? How does the personalized nature of the Latin American caudillo make some of the problems worse?

IMPORTANT WORDS
AND CONCEPTS

reconcentration

"Remember the *Maine!*"

Platt Amendment

Guantanamo Bay
 (Gwan-'tah-nah-moh)

Radio Rebelde (Ray-'bel-day)

Movimiento de 26 Julio
 (Moh-bee-mee-'en-toh,
 'Hoo-lyoh)

Bay of Pigs

Chapter 13   **CHILE**

IN THIS CHAPTER YOU WILL DISCOVER:

That certain economic problems have persisted in Chile since 1935

What programs were proposed to help the rural and urban poor in Chile

What happened to the first elected Marxist government in the Western Hemisphere

KEY QUESTIONS

1. What created Chile's economic problems? How did Eduardo Frei Montalva propose to restructure both the agricultural and industrial sectors?

2. Why were some segments of Chilean society concerned about the election of Salvador Allende? Describe the reactions to this election as indicated by an American reporter.

3. What steps did Allende take to improve Chile's economic situation? Indicate how many of these programs resulted in further economic crises. Why did both conservatives and Marxists criticize Allende?

4. What were the immediate results of the army coup under Augusto Pinochet? Cite ways in which the Central Intelligence Agency of the United States apparently participated in Chilean politics.

5. How did the Pinochet government attempt to eliminate Marxism?

IMPORTANT PEOPLE

Eduardo Frei Montalva
  (Eh-'doahr-doh Fray
  Mohn-'tahl-vah)

Salvador Allende Gossens
  (Sahl-vah-'dor Ah-'yen-day
  'Gaw-sens)

Augusto Pinochet Ugarte
  (Ah-'goo-stoh Pee-no-'chet
  Oo-'gahr-tay)

**IMPORTANT WORDS
AND CONCEPTS**

Unidad Popular (Oo-nee-'dahd
  Poh-pew-'lahr)

Socialists

Communists

Radical party

Christian Democrats

inflation

Chapter 14   **ARGENTINA**

IN THIS CHAPTER YOU WILL DISCOVER:

How Argentine leaders have attempted to solve problems in land and urban development

What strengths and weaknesses marked Juan Perón's long rule in Argentine politics

IMPORTANT PEOPLE

Bernardino Rivadavia
  (Ber-nahr-'dhee-noh
  Ree-vah-'dah-vyah)

Julio A. Roca ('Hoo-lyoh 'Roh-kah)

KEY QUESTIONS

1. Describe the conditions in Argentina that promoted latifundism.

2. What convinced Juan Perón that dictatorship was the best form of government? Which Argentinians became Perón's main supporters?

3. How did Perón maintain his position? Indicate how Perón's policies produced economic and political problems for his government.

4. How was Perón able to return to power in Argentina? Describe his political base. In what ways did Perón's wives Evita and Isabel represent unusual political roles for Latin American women? How did the Perón era end?

5. How did the Falkland Islands War influence politics in Argentina? What problems has the Alfonsín government faced?

Chapter 15   **BRAZIL**

IN THIS CHAPTER YOU WILL DISCOVER:

What issues underlay the abolition of the Brazilian monarchy

What continuing economic concerns have occupied dictators in Brazil

How the development policies of Kubitschek, Goulart, and the military met with mixed success

The provisions of the 1988 constitution

KEY QUESTIONS

1. Which key powers, as described in the Constitution of 1823, did Dom Pedro I reserve for himself? Which issues caused Brazilians to become dissatisfied with Dom Pedro's decisions? What segments of the population demonstrated their ability to unite and force the abdication of the emperor?

Domingo Faustino Sarmiento
(Doh-'meeng-go Fau-'stee-no Sahr-'myayn-toh)

Juan Domingo Perón (Hwahn Doh-'meen-go Pay-'rohn)

Eva Duarte de Perón ('Ay-vah 'Dwahr-tay)

Isabel Martinez de Perón ('Ee-sah-bel Mar-'tee-nes)

Raúl Alfonsín
(Rah-'ool Ahl-fohn-'seen)

IMPORTANT WORDS AND CONCEPTS

descamisados
(days-kah-mee-'sah-dohs)

La Prensa (Lah 'Pren-sah)

Peronism

junta ('hoon-tah)

IMPORTANT PEOPLE

Dom Pedro I (Dohm 'Pay-dro)

Dom Pedro II

Getulio Vargas (Hay-'too-lee-oh 'Vahr-guhs)

Juscelino Kubitschek
(Hoo-seh-'lee-noh 'Koo-buh-chek)

Oscar Niemeyer ('Nee-my-er)

João Goulart (Zhwou'[n] Goo-'lar)

José Sarney
(Hoh-'zay 'Sahr-nee)

2. Explain how Dom Pedro II offended both liberals and conservatives by his policies.

3. How did the Brazilian method of selecting a president involve politicans in the provinces? Describe the economic policy of Getulio Vargas. List three conditions that brought Vargas's rule to an end.

4. How did Juscelino Kubitschek promote Brazilian nationalism? What part did Brasília play in this development?

5. Why did João Goulart's assumption of the presidency concern the Brazilian army and the conservatives? Why did the army attempt to control Goulart?

6. Describe how Goulart's land reform policies created economic problems.

7. What achievements indicate that Brazil has a stable civilian government?

IMPORTANT WORDS AND CONCEPTS

industrialization

Brasília (Brah-'see-lee-ah)

civil liberties

Chapter 16 RELATIONS WITH THE UNITED STATES

IN THIS CHAPTER YOU WILL DISCOVER:

How the United States influenced Latin American politics

What benefits and liabilities resulted from American intervention

How certain factors changed the United States' attitude toward Latin America

What mutual problems presently concern the United States and Latin America

KEY QUESTIONS

1. List the reasons why the United States and Great Britain wished to keep other European nations out of Latin America. Why did the United States not join with Great Britain in issuing a declaration like the Monroe Doctrine?

2. Discuss the occasions when the United States intervened in Latin America to enforce the Monroe Doctrine or the Platt Amendment.

3. In what ways did the United States' methods of building the

IMPORTANT PEOPLE

James Monroe

John Quincy Adams

Theodore Roosevelt

Dr. Francois Duvalier
   (Fran-'swah Doo-val-ee-'yah)

Jean-Claude Duvalier
   (Jahn-Clohd Doo-val-ee'yah)

Franklin D. Roosevelt

Manuel Noriega
   (Man-'well Nor-ee-'ay-gah)

John F. Kennedy

Oscar Romero
   (Os-'car Roh-'may-roh)

Anastasio Somoza
   (Ah-nah-'stah-see-yoh Sah-'moh-zah)

Jesús T. Piñero (Hay-'soos
   Pee-'nyeh-roh)

Luis Muñoz Marín (Loo-'ees
   'Moo-nyohs Mah-'reen)

Panama Canal demonstrate interference in the affairs of Latin American governments?

4. How did President Theodore Roosevelt broaden the powers of the Monroe Doctrine through the Roosevelt Corollary? What effect did this have on relations between Haiti and the United States?

5. Indicate the difference between the Good Neighbor Policy of Franklin Roosevelt and the Monroe Doctrine and the Roosevelt Corollary. Give specific examples of American action in Latin America that demonstrate this difference.

6. What were the goals of the Pan American Union and the Organization of American States? How did the United States' role in Europe following World War II influence the creation of the Inter-American Development Bank?

7. What condition in Latin America brought about the organization of the Alliance for Progress? List the goals of the Alliance. What did the Alliance actually accomplish?

8. What has been the role of the United States government in the conflicts in El Salvador, Nicaragua, and Grenada?

9. Why did extensive foreign investment in Puerto Rico cause social problems for many of its inhabitants?

10. Outline the structure of government in Puerto Rico and the relationship between Puerto Rico and the United States.

11. How did Governor Luis Muñoz Marín propose to meet Puerto Rico's need for development? Which issues still cause concern among Puerto Ricans today?

IMPORTANT WORDS AND CONCEPTS

Monroe Doctrine

Platt Amendment

Panama Canal

Roosevelt Corollary to the Monroe Doctrine

Good Neighbor Policy

Pan American Union

Organization of American States

Inter-American Development Bank

Alianza Para el Progresso (Ah-lee-'ahn-sah 'Pah-rah el Pro-'gray-so)

Sandinistas (Sahn-din-'ees-tahs)

contras ('cohn-tras)

dependency

commonwealth

"Operation Bootstrap"

Chapter 17 **CONFRONTING CURRENT PROBLEMS**

IN THIS CHAPTER YOU WILL DISCOVER:

What demands poverty and increasing population make on Latin Americans

How poverty shapes the lives of some Ecuadorian Indians

How some Latin Americans use violence to try to change their society

IMPORTANT WORDS AND CONCEPTS

job-producing investments

campos ('kahm-pohs)

Quechua ('Kay-chwah)

cantón (kahn-'tohn)

patrón (pah-'trohn)

KEY QUESTIONS

1. How does the lack of money to build factories and to provide new jobs in Latin America keep much of the population poor? In what ways do foreign investments contribute to this condition? How does the current system of agriculture hinder development?

2. Indicate ways in which the daily lives of Ecuadorian Indians demonstrate the harshness of their poverty. What other classes of Latin Americans do these Indians describe? What is the relationship between the Indians and these other Latin American peoples?

3. How does Latin America's rapidly increasing population heighten economic and social problems?

4. State the goal of the Arias Peace Plan. Explain how cooperation on other problems can be an advantage for Latin America.

5. What evidence can you cite that indicates that some people try to solve Latin America's problems through the use of violence?

quinoa (kee-'noh-ah)

campesinos (kahm-pay-'see-nohs)

cholos ('choh-lohs)

chicheria (chee-chay-'ree-ah)

hucksters

price controls

Arias Peace Plan

IMPORTANT PEOPLE

Oscar Arias Sanchez
  (Ohs-'car Ar-ee-'ahs
  Sahn-'che!.z)